Ancient Persia

JOHN CURTIS

HARVARD UNIVERSITY PRESS
Cambridge, Massachusetts
1990

Photo acknowledgements
British Library 42–3, 77–8, 84
John Curtis 5, 9, 23, 25, 28, 39,
76, 85
Vesta Curtis 2, 12, 38
Georgina Herrmann contents
page, 41, 46, 49–51
Deutsches Archäologisches
Institut, Abteilung Tehran 44.

Front cover Model chariot in gold from the Oxus Treasure, pulled by four small horses or ponies. Can be compared with the chariot shown on cylinder seal **56**. Achaemenid period, 5th–4th century BC. L 18.8 cm.

Back cover Part of a polychrome glazed brick frieze from Susa showing a procession of guards in Persian costume, perhaps the 'Immortals' who made up the king's personal bodyguard. The panel has been extensively restored, and dates from the reign of Darius (522–486BC). On permanent loan to the British Museum from the Musée du Louvre. Ht 199 cm.

Inside front cover Persepolis relief showing one of a pair of winged sphinxes originally flanking a winged disc. From Darius' Palace, south stairs. Ht 82.1 cm.

Inside back cover Embossed gold plaque from the Oxus Treasure, in the shape of a fabulous creature with the body of a winged stag and the head of a horned lion. There are two long pointed projections at the back for attachment. 5th–3rd century BC. W 6.15 cm.

Title page Silver dish, partially gilded, showing a Sasanian king, probably Shapur II (AD309–79), hunting stags. D 18.0 cm.

This page View of the ruins of Persepolis from the hill (Kuh-i Ramat) to the east.

Contents

Preface page 4

Preface

To many Europeans the word Persia is evocative of beautiful works of art – carpets, tiles, fine ceramics, miniatures and metal-work. Or they might think of Persian poets such as Hafez, Saadi or Omar Khayyam, who are often quoted in translation. Yet these artistic and literary accomplishments all date from the Islamic era. Much less well known, but no less fascinating, are the art and history of ancient Persia, or Iran, and it is these that form the subject of this book.

In a short work such as this it is obviously impossible to deal comprehensively with the civilisation of ancient Persia, so I have tried to concentrate on those aspects that are likely to be of interest to the general reader while at the same time providing a coherent account. To some extent this book is written around the British Museum collections, and I hope it will also provide a useful guide to them.

In the preparation of this account I had help from my wife Vesta Curtis, whom I have consulted on a number of points and who has also typed the manuscript. I am also extremely grateful to Georgina Herrmann and Michael Roaf, who read the text and made a number of helpful suggestions, usually but not always incorporated. Needless to say, any inaccuracies or inadequacies that remain are my own responsibility. Thanks are also due to Barbara Winter of the British Museum Photographic Service.

1 The land of Iran

Iran is a land of extraordinary diversity, geographically, climatically and ethnically. The central part of the country is a great plateau, mostly between 1000 and 2000 m above sea level, situated between the Caspian Sea in the north and the Persian Gulf and the Gulf of Oman in the south. In the central and eastern parts of the plateau are two great salt deserts, the Dasht-i Lut and the Dasht-i Kavir. These are dried-up former lakes, where settlement is practically impossible. On the west, Iran is divided from the lowland plains of Mesopotamia by the high Zagros mountains, and in the north the Elburz range, with the majestic peak of Demavend in the centre, separates Tehran from the Caspian Sea. In the north-east the Khorasan Mountains, an extension of the Elburz chain, form a barrier between the plateau and what is now Soviet Turkmenistan. To the east the boundaries between Iran and Afghanistan and Pakistan respectively are less well defined, but here too there are mountain ranges marking the eastern edge of the Iranian plateau.

In a land the size of Iran there are, naturally, many regional variations in scenery and climate. Khuzistan in the south-west, for example, is essentially an extension of the lowland plains of Mesopotamia and enjoys the same warm, arid climate. In the north the strip of land around the Caspian Sea is clothed with dense, jungle-like vegetation that thrives in the sub-tropical climate. In Sistan, a depression centred on Lake Hamun on the Afghan border, the stifling heat of summer and the high winds make living conditions very unpleasant. However, most of the plateau enjoys a pleasant continental climate, warm but not intolerably hot in the summer and with snow for two to three months in the winter.

Modern Iran is composed of many diverse

1 Map of Iran showing the principal ancient sites and modern towns mentioned in the text.

2 The village of Malyan in Fars, showing mud-brick houses of the same type as were built in antiquity. Many aspects of village life have remained unchanged for centuries.

ethnic elements. In addition to Persians, who form the largest group, there are Turks, Kurds, Lurs, Baluchis and Arabs, as well as a number of ethnic minorities. This must also have been the situation in antiquity, with the country occupied by different groups with different backgrounds and speaking different languages. This is reflected in the archaeological record, which shows evidence of different cultures often with their own distinctive art styles. In antiquity Iran was not a homogeneous unit, and contacts were not confined to the borders of modern Iran. For example, at different periods south-east Iran had close connections with Afghanistan; Khuzistan (part of ancient Elam) had close connections with Mesopotamia, and north-western Iran

(Azerbaijan) had links with the cultures of the Caucasus. Not until the Achaemenid period (550–330BC) was the country united in a meaningful sense, and even then the society was probably very mixed, allowing for the continuation of local art-styles and traditions.

The name Iran is of ancient origin, meaning 'land of the Aryans'; in his famous inscription at Bisitun, Darius refers to himself as an Aryan, and the Sasanian kings use the term 'Eranshahr', but this covered an area much greater than that of modern Iran. Although the name Persia should properly be used to describe one part of the country only, namely the modern province of Fars (ancient Parsa or Greek Persis), it is often used by Europeans to describe the whole land of Iran.

2 The early periods

3 Pottery bowl with dark brown painted decoration on a buff background, showing birds and geometric motifs. From Susa, late 4th millennium BC. On permanent loan to the British Museum from the Musée du Louvre. Ht 20.5 cm.

Although the very early history of man in Iran goes back well beyond the Neolithic period, in this book we pick up the story at that time – around 6000BC – when people no longer eked out an existence solely by hunting wild animals and gathering plants and fruit, but had begun to domesticate animals and plant wheat and barley. The number of settled communities increased, particularly in the eastern Zagros mountains, and handmade painted pottery appears at sites such as Tepe Guran in Luristan and Ali Kosh in Khuzistan, although at Ganj Dareh near Kermanshah, lightly fired pottery probably dates from as early as the late eighth millennium BC.

Throughout the prehistoric period, from the middle of the sixth millennium BC to about 3000BC, painted pottery is a characteristic feature of many sites in Iran. Forms and decoration differ in various parts of the country, but often common traits can be observed. Sometimes similarities can be found with the pottery from neighbouring Mesopotamia to the west, but generally these pottery vessels are distinctive local products that owe much to the inspiration of local potters. The decorative effect is often remarkable, and represents a high level of artistic achievement. The history of the development of this pottery is complex, but some general observations can be made.

In the earlier part of this long period, often known as Chalcolithic, the most distinctive pottery is red or buff ware, painted in black with geometric designs often in combination with cross-hatching. But the high point in the development of prehistoric Iranian painted pottery comes in the fourth millennium BC, with a greater frequency of animal designs combined with a wide variety of geometric motifs. This pottery, now sometimes made on a wheel, is found at places such as Tepe Sialk near Kashan, Tepe Hissar near Damghan, Tall-i Bakun near Persepolis and the great

4 Pottery bowl with brown painted decoration on a cream background, showing bird-headed men and stylised Maltese crosses. Thought to be from Tall-i Bakun near Persepolis. Late 5th–early 4th millennium BC.

contributions to the history and prehistory of Iran. The journeys were carried out under the auspices of Harvard University and the British Museum, and the material not required by law to stay in Iran was divided between those two institutions.

Sir Aurel Stein's pioneering work in south-eastern Iran paved the way for a survey undertaken by Harvard University in 1967, which led to the discovery of Tepe Yahya. This site, in Kerman province, is one of a number of urban communities which, by the late fourth millennium BC, had become sufficiently highly organised to need written administrative records. They used clay tablets, written in a pictographic script known as proto-Elamite, and examples have been found at a number of other sites in Iran such as Tepe Sialk, Shahr-i Sokhteh, possibly Godin Tepe and, most 5 notably, Susa.

Undoubtedly the most interesting level at Tepe Yahya, though, is later, dating from about the mid third millennium BC (level IVB 1). There were no permanent structures in this level, but extensive evidence for the carving of artefacts in chlorite, a soft greyish-green stone. Vessels fashioned from this have been found as far apart as Mesopotamia and Bactria, and 6 Oman and Bahrain in the Persian Gulf, as well as at Susa. One centre of production – although not the only one – for chlorite vessels was Tepe Yahya. In the repertoire of chlorite objects, straight-sided bowls were particularly popular, and favourite designs include monstrous snakes with lions'(?) heads, birds of prey, and the façade of a building perhaps meant to be a temple. Clearly the chlorite vessels manufactured at Tepe Yahya travelled far afield, and some no doubt found their way to Susa and sites in Mesopotamia.

These connections with the west are also attested at Shahr-i Sokhteh, a site east of the Dasht-i Lut in Sistan near the Afghan-Iranian border. Excavations here were conducted by

mound of Susa in Khuzistan. It includes bowls, jars, goblets and footed beakers that are usually in cream or buff ware, with the designs in black or dark brown paint. Among the animals, which are either in panels or arranged in rows, are goats with large circular horns and waisted bodies; crane-like birds with long legs and necks; leopards; and dogs with long thin bodies, possibly the forerunners of modern salukis. Occasionally human figures are also shown.

Many painted potsherds, which are of great interest to scholars and students of ancient Iran, are now in the reserve collections of the British Museum. They were collected by Sir Aurel Stein (1862–1943), who has been described as 'the most prodigious combination of scholar, explorer, archaeologist and geographer of his generation'. In the course of four journeys in Iran between 1932 and 1936, Stein visited many sites in Kerman, Baluchistan, Fars and western Iran. At some of these sites Stein made test trenches and limited excavations; in this way he made valuable

5 The reconstructed remains of Period v at Godin Tepe, late 4th millennium BC.

an Italian expedition led by Maurizio Tosi. From the extensive graveyard and in the adjoining settlement there is evidence that Shahr-i Sokhteh was trading in semi-precious stones and other raw materials: many beads of turquoise, lapis lazuli and chlorite have been found, and in one grave was a set of copper and stone tools as well as three blocks of lapis lazuli ready to be worked; thousands of lapis lazuli beads were found in an industrial area.

There are great quantities of lapis lazuli in Mesopotamia, too, at this time, notably at sites like Ur, which are presumed to have originated from the mines of Sar-i Sang in the Badakh-shan area of Afghanistan. This lapis probably came to Mesopotamia by way of sites like Shahr-i Sokhteh, although this was certainly not the only route – much lapis lazuli has been found, for example, at Tepe Hissar. Echoes of sites such as Tepe Yahya, which produced chlorite, and Shahr-i Sokhteh, which was an important post on one of the lapis lazuli routes, are perhaps to be found in the Sumerian literary references to Marhashi and Aratta, fabulous places far away to the east which were sources of valuable stones and metals as well as exotic animals and plants.

At the end of the third millennium, around

6 (*Left*) Two fragments of a chlorite vessel showing a hero struggling with a caprid (left, 6.5 cm wide) and a long-necked monster with lion's head (right, 8.5 cm wide). Inscribed on the back with the name of the Akkadian king Rimush (*c.*2278–2270BC). Although found at Ur in Mesopotamia, the fragments clearly derive from Iran.

2000BC, there seems to have been a flourishing civilisation in south-east Iran which still had connections with Elam to the west, although less so with Mesopotamia, but also with southern Bactria (northern Afghanistan) to the north-east. At this time Tepe Yahya reached its maximum extent and was at its most prosperous. But the most remarkable site of this period is Shahdad in the Dasht-i Lut, about 60 km east of Kerman, excavated by the Iranian archaeologist Ali Hakemi. A wealth of material of extraordinary diversity and unexpected richness was found in cemetery areas near here. Amongst the outstanding finds are an extraordinary standard comprising a copper plaque, showing an enthroned figure in the centre with supplementary scenes all around, mounted on a long metal rod surmounted by a bird of prey; some large statues in unbaked clay of male figures, represented from the waist upwards; a variety of vessels in chlorite, alabaster and copper; and cylinder

and stamp seals. Clearly the graves span much, if not all, of the third millennium BC, but the richest are the latest in the series. From late graves come at least three copper alloy axes with crescent-shaped blades and elaborate crests behind the shaft-hole. These axes from Shahdad are very similar to two axes now in the British Museum from a cemetery near Khinaman, about 120 km west of Shahdad. As well as being similar in form to the axes from Shahdad, the Khinaman examples are also made of arsenical copper, that is arsenic (rather than tin) has been added to the copper to make it a harder and more suitable alloy. Analyses of material from other sites show that the use of arsenical copper was widespread at this time, particularly in south-east Iran. The Khinaman and Shahdad axes can be closely dated because just such an axe is shown on a seal-impression from Susa belonging to the period *c.*1950–1900BC. Actual examples of such axes are known from Bactria

8 Bronze axe with silver inlay, showing a tiger attacking a goat. The tiger is in turn being molested by a boar. As the blade is blunt and there is no proper provision for a sturdy handle, this axe was probably ceremonial. It was obtained in the North-West Provinces of India (now Pakistan) but may originally have come from Bactria. Related to the axes from Khinaman 7, it may also date from *c.*2000BC. Analysis has shown that the alloy is copper with approximately 10% tin and 1–3% arsenic. Given to the British Museum in 1913 by Henry Oppenheimer through the National Art Collections Fund. L 17.8 cm.

8 (northern Afghanistan), although these axes are mostly without precise provenance. There are also many other points of contact with this area, such as compartmented stamp seals.

Around 2000BC there was clearly a prosperous and flourishing civilisation in south-east Iran, represented at places such as Shahdad, Khinaman and Tepe Yahya. There was some contact with Elam, but connections seem to have been strongest with northern Afghanistan. This has led one scholar to regard south-east Iran and western central Asia as a single cultural zone which he calls 'Turan'. However that may be, it is obvious that there was in the Kerman area at this time a rich, distinctive culture about which we know little. No doubt there are many more towns and cemeteries of this date waiting to be discovered in this part of Iran.

After about 1900BC, the splendid civilisations in eastern Iran seem to have declined and the archaeological record in the area becomes correspondingly sparse. Such was not the case, though, in western Iran. There is, for example, a long sequence of monochrome

7 (*Above*) Two ceremonial axes *c.*2000BC from a cemetery at Khinaman near Kerman. They were obtained by Sir Percy Sykes together with a collection of vessels, pins, lanceheads, a dagger and a scraper, mostly of arsenical copper. A raised oval shape on the shaft-hole of each axe might represent an eye. W (of top axe) 12.4 cm, (of bottom axe) 13.0 cm.

9 (*Above*) The mound of Tepe Giyan near Nahavand in Luristan. Traces can still be seen of Professor Roman Ghirshman's 1930s excavations; fertile countryside surrounds the site.

10 (*Right*) Pottery jar decorated with dark brown paint on a buff background. The design includes stylised birds. Obtained in Nahavand, allegedly from Tepe Giyan, *c*.2000BC. Ht 27.6 cm.

painted pottery stretching down to the middle of the second millennium BC at sites such as Tepe Giyan near Nahavand, and Godin Tepe. This pottery, generally painted in dark brown on a buff background, bears an interesting range of intricate geometric designs, often with the addition of birds. But this is only one of a number of different styles of pottery current in western Iran at this time. Around Lake Urmia, for instance, a distinctive painted pottery shows connections with Transcaucasia. Birds and geometric designs – commonly triangles – characterise this pottery, which is painted in black or in black and cream on a red background. Many examples have been found at Haftavan Tepe, excavated by Charles Burney, and there is a fine piece now in the British Museum.

3 Elam

Elam is the name given to the south-western part of Iran in antiquity. It includes not only the lowland area corresponding to modern Khuzistan, with the great site of Susa, but also the highland areas to the north and east, up to and including Tall-i Malyan (ancient Anshan) in Fars, just 43 km west of Persepolis. Because of its geographical position, being an extension of the alluvial plains of Mesopotamia, lowland Susa was sometimes brought within the cultural orbit of Mesopotamia, but in the highland areas Elamite traditions and culture were more carefully guarded. At certain times the lowland area dominated the surrounding highlands, but at other periods the initiative came from the upland areas and the lowland zone, or Susiana, was removed from Mesopotamian influence.

For many years Susa was regarded as the capital of Elam, but it is now clear that it was only one of several major centres, another being Anshan. Nevertheless, Susa remains the best-known and certainly the most extensively excavated site in Elam, which has to some extent distorted our picture of the region as a whole. Susa was visited by a number of early travellers, but proper excavations did not begin until 1850–52. These were carried out by officers of the Turko-Persian Boundary Commission, chiefly William Kennet Loftus (1820–58), who is perhaps better known for his later work at Warka, Nimrud and Nineveh in Mesopotamia.

Colonel H. C. Rawlinson, the British consul at Baghdad and one of the pioneers in the decipherment of cuneiform, trusted that within a few months of starting his 1852 campaign Loftus 'would have laid the great mound of Susa completely bare', but according to his own account Loftus was more cautious and viewed the prospect of working at Susa with some trepidation: 'On looking around the vast area of mounds, and considering the small sum at my disposal for the investigation of their contents, I was almost tempted to regard my enterprize as a hopeless one.' Nevertheless, he was able partially to expose and plan an Achaemenid-period apadana or columned hall, as well as finding some glazed bricks and miscellaneous antiquities from earlier periods. Since 1884 Susa has been a French preserve, and they have continued to work there until recently. The roll-call of distinguished French archaeologists who have excavated at Susa includes Marcel Dieulafoy, Jacques de Morgan and Roman Ghirshman. The French have also left an impressive landmark at the site with what must be the most sumptuous dig-house ever constructed for archaeological work in the Middle East: a castle, constructed from materials found in the ruins and known as the 'Château'. The findings of the French archaeologists are many, including a large number of spectacular pieces.

As mentioned earlier, clay tablets written in proto-Elamite script and dating from around 3000BC or a little before are known from a number of sites in Iran, including Susa. In the latter part of the third millennium, lowland

11 An engraving showing the mound of Susa, after a sketch by H. A. Churchill, an artist who drew some of the material found in Loftus' excavations. The prominent building at the front of the mound is, according to local tradition, the tomb of the prophet Daniel.

Elam was dominated by the Akkadian, and later the Third Dynasty of Ur kings in Mesopotamia. After the collapse of the Ur Dynasty, 'Greater Elam' became an independent state, but in the first half of the second millennium local dynasts continued to use the Sumerian and Akkadian languages for administrative texts and other inscriptions. This is illustrated by two objects in the British Museum collection, a bronze axe and a bronze beaker with large handle. Both bear inscriptions of Adda-hushu, a ruler of Susa around 1900BC, written in a curious mixture of Sumerian and Akkadian that is typical of Elamite royal inscriptions.

At the same time, however, some aspects of Elamite culture are quite distinctive. There is, for example, the attractive pottery known as 'kaftari ware', usually buff and painted with rows of birds (*kaftar* means pigeon in Persian).

The type-site for this pottery is now Tall-i Malyan, excavated between 1971 and 1978 by William Sumner on behalf of the University Museum in Philadelphia, Pennsylvania. And already at this time, in the first part of the second millennium, there are examples of the rock-reliefs (at Kurangun and Naqsh-i Rustam) that are later familiar features of Elamite art.

The heyday of the Elamite state came during what is known as the Middle Elamite period (*c*.1450–1100BC). Inscriptions were now written in Elamite (a language that is still only partially understood and has no known relatives), and many original works of art were produced. Many of the most impressive of these come from Susa and are now on display in the Louvre Museum in Paris.

Elamite metal-work was particularly accomplished. There are, for example, a life-size

13 (*Above*) A pendant of pale blue chalcedony, pierced for suspension, with an inscription in Elamite. The text records that the 12th-century king Shilhak-Inshushinak had the stone engraved for his daughter Bar-Uli, and the accompanying scene shows him presenting it to her. This sort of personal touch is only rarely found in the art of Iran and neighbouring countries. L 4.0 cm.

bronze statue of Napirisha, wife of the thirteenth-century BC ruler Untash-Napirisha, weighing 1750 kg, and a model in bronze of a religious ceremony made for Shilhak-Inshushinak in the twelfth century BC. Then there is a spectacular cache of objects found beneath the Temple of Inshushinak, built by this same ruler. Amongst these are figurines of gold and silver, each showing a figure (probably the king) carrying a goat, which he is presumably about to offer for sacrifice, and a whetstone terminating in a gold lion's head. These objects are sometimes regarded as foundation deposits, but this remains an open question.

The Middle Elamite period also witnessed the production of many terracotta figurines. An interesting group of these was found by Loftus at Susa: he refers to a collection of about 200, some forty of which are now in the British Museum, the greater number of them being 'nude representations of the goddess'. A closely comparable figurine has been found at the site of Haft Tepe, also in Khuzistan, excavated by E. O. Negahban (then of the University of Tehran). Haft Tepe was occupied, it seems, only during the fourteenth to thirteenth centuries BC, so any material found there can be relatively closely dated. Two bitumen roundels in the British Museum are of the same type as one found at Haft Tepe, and can therefore be ascribed to the same period.

Among the many other interesting finds from Haft Tepe are several clay heads with inlaid eyes. But the most extraordinary feature about the site is that it appears to have been a complex consisting only of religious buildings and tombs, and may have been founded specifically as a centre of some funerary cult. In this respect it closely resembles Chogha Zanbil, a site 40 km south-east of Susa, which was founded by Untash-Napirisha possibly after Haft Tepe had been abandoned. This may also have been a religious centre, as there is a ziggurat or temple tower at the site

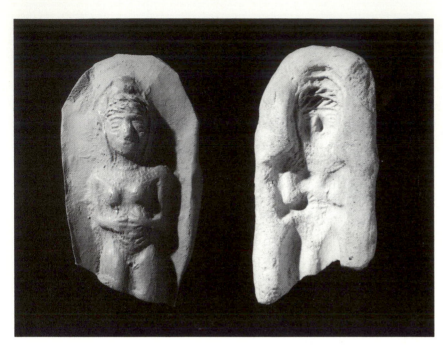

15 (*Above*) Terracotta mould (right) for making clay figurines, from the excavations of W. K. Loftus at Susa. On the left is a modern impression from this mould. Probably Middle Elamite period, 14th–13th century BC. Ht 9.9 cm.

16 (*Left*) Bronze figure thought to represent a fish-tailed goddess, perhaps originally fitted on to the armrest of a throne. Allegedly obtained near Tang-i Sarvak. The hairstyle of the figure may be compared with that of the terracotta figurines from Susa 14, and like them this piece probably dates from the Middle Elamite period. Ht 12.0 cm.

along with various other shrines and temples.

Amongst the architectural ornaments found at Chogha Zanbil were wall plaques of glazed pottery, one of which has been presented to the British Museum by the excavator, Roman Ghirshman. He also presented two small fragments of glass rod which, set in diagonal panels, were used to decorate doors. These rods were of dark blue or black glass with white spiral bands.

From Chogha Zanbil, as indeed also from Susa, have come many interesting cylinder seals, often made of faience (glazed quartz composition) and sometimes glass. Unlike earlier seals from Elam which are closely related to Mesopotamian types, those of the Middle Elamite period show evidence of local inspiration. A distinctive feature of these seals is a ladder pattern at either end of the cylinder.

Towards the end of the Middle Elamite period, in 1168BC, the Elamite king Shutruk-Nahhunte invaded southern Mesopotamia and took back to Susa many important monuments, including the Code of Hammurabi. But the tables were turned when, towards the end of the twelfth century BC, Nebuchadnezzar I of Babylon (1125–1104BC) invaded Elamite territory and brought to an abrupt close this flourishing period in the history of Elam. Thereafter, historical sources fall silent for several centuries.

But we do know that Elamite artistic traditions continued to flourish in the Neo-Elamite period (c.1100–550BC). There are, for example, rock carvings at Shikaft-i Salman and at Kul-i Farah on the edge of the Izeh plain. Both sets of reliefs appear to belong to outdoor sanctuaries where religious ceremonies would have been held. Those at Kul-i Farah show just such a ceremony taking place, with a procession, a sacrifice and a banquet. Musical accompaniment is provided by stringed instruments and drums. The inscriptions on these reliefs clearly date from the Neo-Elamite period, but some art historians have suggested that the reliefs themselves were executed in the Middle Elamite period. But even if this is true, the sanctuaries were obviously in use during the later period as well. Polychrome glazed bricks, which first appeared in the Middle Elamite period, continued to be produced, and there are interesting examples showing mythological beasts dating from about the eighth century BC.

In the seventh century BC, Elam became increasingly embroiled with the powerful Assyrian state to the west. This struggle is graphically illustrated in a magnificent series of reliefs from Nineveh in the British Museum, particularly those showing Ashurbanipal's campaign against Te-Umman and the rout of the Elamites at Til-Tiba on the Ulai river. In 646 BC, Ashurbanipal marched into the eastern districts of Elam and returned to sack Susa with great ferocity. Elam's days as a power to be reckoned with were now over.

It is sometimes suggested that Elam is nothing more than an extension of lowland Mesopotamia, and that its art and architecture are entirely derivative from Mesopotamian prototypes. However, although it is true that lowland Elam was at times prey to Mesopotamian influence, this is much less the case in the highland areas and, as we have seen, at certain times – notably during the Middle Elamite period – the material culture of Elam can be sharply differentiated from that of Mesopotamia.

17 (*Above*) Glazed pottery wall plaque from Chogha Zanbil, inscribed with the name of the 13th-century BC ruler Untash-Napirisha. Presented to the British Museum by Professor R. Ghirshman. *c.*37.5 cm square.

18 (*Right*) Two bitumen discs encircled by copper bands. The decorated surfaces were originally overlaid with silver gilt, which survives intact for one example but has been removed from the bitumen disc. The gold leaf was attached to the silver by burnishing and heating, a process known as diffusion bonding. These discs may have decorated horse harness or been mounted on double baldrics and worn on the chest. Middle Elamite, 14th–13th century BC. D 8.2 cm (top disc), and 9.8 cm.

4 The age of migrations

In the second half of the second millennium BC, from about 1400BC onwards, new pottery forms appear, mainly at sites in north-western Iran and on the southern slopes of the Elburz mountains. The most characteristic variety of this new pottery, which is found alongside red and buff forms, ranges in colour from light grey to black and is usually called Early Western Grey Ware, or Iron I. The surface is almost always burnished, often giving the vessel a bright sheen and making it very smooth to the touch, sometimes giving it a soapy feel. Sites where this pottery has been found include Hasanlu, Dinkha Tepe, Qeytari-yeh in the northern suburbs of Tehran, Khorvin, Tepe Sialk and Tepe Giyan.

The most typical shapes are large pouring vessels with a long horizontal spout (some-times called beak-spouted vessels); tripods; goblets with pedestal bases, sometimes very large with a handle at the side; cups with single handles; simple bowls, sometimes with pedestal bases; and large basins with flared sides. Occasionally this pottery is elaborately decorated, so that vessels with handle and long spout might have birds' or animals' heads, sometimes highly stylised, on a projection at the back of the spout.

With the exception of Hasanlu, grey ware pots have usually been found in cemeteries situated outside the settlements to which they belong. The bodies were often placed in simple graves, but sometimes they were put in tombs built of mud-brick or more rarely stone. The bodies were accompanied by a selection of pots, usually about half-a-dozen depending on the wealth of the deceased, as well as weapons (often a dagger or spear) and jewellery such as bracelets, earrings, beads and pins, which were worn by both men and women. At this period weapons are always made of bronze, with iron (paradoxically in view of the termin-ology) not actually making its appearance until the Iron II period.

It is sometimes thought that the appearance of this grey ware pottery in western Iran signifies the first arrival there of the Iranians, forebears of the people who appear later in historical sources as the Medes and the Per-sians. They are mentioned first during the reign of the Assyrian king Shalmaneser III (858–824BC), who campaigned in western Iran. It is supposed that these people, who spoke Indo-European languages, were not indigenous to Iran – their homeland is thought to have been somewhere in the vast expanse of steppeland that stretched from the river Danube east to the Ural mountains. It is assumed, through a combination of linguistic evidence and much later written sources, that they entered Iran from the north-east, so they would have come down the east side of the Caspian Sea.

The Iron Age grey wares of western Iran appear to be derived from the earlier Late Bronze Age grey wares found at sites such as Tepe Hissar and Tureng Tepe, near the south-east corner of the Caspian Sea. At sites in western Iran where grey ware has been found there is a sudden break from earlier pottery traditions, and taken together these facts could indicate that people using grey ware pottery arrived in western Iran from the east. The Late Bronze Age grey wares of north-east Iran themselves belong to a tradition that stretches back to the late third millennium BC, and they may be compared with pottery found in Turkmenistan at sites such as Namazga-Depe. Another point of contact is that pins with double-spiral heads have been found both in Turkmenistan and at Tepe Hissar. It is possible, therefore, that the Iranians moved into the area to the south-east of the Caspian Sea from Turkmenistan in the late third millennium BC, and thence spread into west-ern Iran in the second half of the second millennium BC.

This is an attractive theory, but the issue is

extremely complex. For example, it is true that new languages were introduced, but does this necessarily imply movement of people on a very large scale? We have no idea of the numbers of people involved in this projected migration, nor do we know anything about how they travelled or what social structure they had. The exact date of their arrival in western Iran may never be satisfactorily resolved; indeed, it is possible that the migration took place over a long period of time, perhaps even extending to many centuries.

Pottery related to the grey ware of north-western and central Iran has been found at the important site of Marlik in Gilan; here, between the Elburz mountains and the Caspian Sea, are wooded hills and valleys with dense vegetation and a warm, humid climate in the summer. As its name implies (*mar* is Persian for snake), snakes abound in the area around Tepe Marlik. At this hilltop site in the Gohar Rud valley, fifty-three tombs were opened by Professor E. O. Negahban of the University of Tehran in 1961–2.

The tombs were constructed of stone, and some contained multiple burials. The variety and richness of the burial goods, now in the Tehran Museum, is astonishing. In addition to large bronze animal figurines, bronze mace-heads and other weapons, cylinder and stamp seals, and two mosaic-glass beakers, there are many figurines in red or grey pottery, usually hollow, of both humans and animals. Especially characteristic of Marlik are hump-backed bulls with the head turning into a pouring spout; these figures, stylised and smoothly finished, have an elegant simplicity. Amongst the human figures, several show naked women with grotesquely enlarged thighs and buttocks, rather like the prehistoric figurines of much earlier date. A well-known pair of figures of a man and a woman are again naked, with pronounced genitals and six toes on each foot. They carry beak-spouted jars on

19 (*Left*) Embossed silver beaker c.1400–1000BC, showing horses in the top register and, in the bottom register, winged lions attacking ibexes. This vessel, of unknown provenance, may be compared with material found at Marlik. Ht 14.0 cm.

20 (*Right*) Hollow pottery figure in red burnished clay representing a woman with grotesquely enlarged thighs and buttocks. Of unknown provenance, but possibly from the Marlik area. A thermoluminescence test has given a date of 10th–7th century BC, but a date in the late 2nd millennium BC is probably more likely. Ht 25.5 cm.

their chests and are again highly stylised, their outlines not unlike the modern sculptures of Henry Moore.

There is a splendid collection of gold, silver and bronze vessels from Marlik; one characteristic form is a beaker with concave sides and bands of geometric decoration, often cable patterns, at top and bottom. Between these are embossed designs, generally representing animals and sometimes mythical beasts such as winged bulls. Also well known from Marlik are spouted vessels in bronze and precious metal, which may be compared with the long-spouted pottery vessels in grey ware that are characteristic of the Iron I period. The fine group of jewellery includes gold quadruple-spiral beads of a type datable to *c*.1350–1050BC. On the whole, the graves at Marlik seem to belong to the Iron I period (*c*.1400–1000BC), but the cemetery may have con-

tinued in use after this time. A few objects, notably a bronze fibula (safety-pin), clearly belong to the Iron II or even Iron III periods. We do not know to whom these tombs at Marlik belong, but it is quite likely that they are the graves of wealthy local princes. Alternatively, it has been suggested that they might have belonged to robber barons, as Marlik is close to the valley of the Sefid Rud, a main line of communication between central Iran and the Caspian Sea. Control of this route might have yielded rich pickings.

At the nearby site of Kaluraz, excavated by Ali Hakemi for the Iranian Archaeological Service in 1967, more tombs with vessels of gold and silver, again now in Tehran, have been discovered. Apparently some occupation was associated with the cemetery here, which was lacking at Marlik, and excavations revealed stone foundations for wooden buildings. Japanese excavations in Gilan, in the Dailaman and Halimehjan districts, have uncovered cemeteries of various dates, with the latest belonging to the Sasanian period (3rd–7th century AD).

Unfortunately, there has also been a great deal of tomb-robbing and illegal excavation in Gilan, and this has resulted in a flood of antiquities appearing on the international art market ascribed to the 'Amlash culture', named after a small village in south-eastern Gilan. To some extent 'Amlash' has become a catch-all description for unprovenanced antiquities, so that while much of this material probably does derive from Gilan, some of it certainly does not.

In the Iron II period (*c*.1000–800BC), grey ware pottery now known as Late Western Grey Ware continues to be found at a number of sites, and some new forms emerge. Typical of this period are bridge-spouted vessels – the same jars with long spouts that are known previously but now with the addition of a bridge between the rim and the spout. These

21 Bridge-spouted jug and tripod in grey burnished pottery from the Iron II period, *c*.1000–800BC. Ht 48.7 cm.

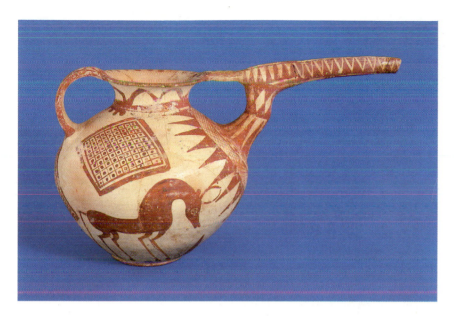

often stood on tripods. Also appearing at this time is an attractive painted pottery, charac- 22 teristically red on cream, principally known from a cemetery at Tepe Sialk. Bridge-spouted jars and other vessels are painted with stylised animals and geometric designs. Hasanlu, a large mound in the Solduz Valley to the south-west of Lake Urmia, is also an important type-site for the grey ware of this date.

The finds at Hasanlu give a unique insight into the culture of north-west Iran in the Iron II period. In the south-west part of the citadel mound a series of four major buildings were arranged around courtyards. In each case the ground-plan is basically the same, consisting of a central hall originally with wooden columns, a pillared entrance, vestibule and spiral stairway on one side and rooms for storage or domestic purposes on the other three sides. These buildings may have been palaces or important administrative buildings or, in one case, a temple. This Level IV at 23 Hasanlu was destroyed by a fierce fire that caused the buildings to collapse, trapping inside them luckless humans as well as a rich assortment of material, some of it from the upper stories of the buildings. Excavations were first undertaken at Hasanlu by Sir Aurel 24 Stein briefly in 1936; by M. Rad and A. Hakemi of the Archaeological Service of Iran in 1947 and 1949; and, most important, by Professor R. H. Dyson of the University Museum in Philadelphia, Pennsylvania, in twelve campaigns between 1957 and 1974. The recent excavators believe that the confla-

22 (*Above left*) Bridge-spouted jug with red decoration on a cream background, showing horned animals and geometric motifs. Allegedly from Tepe Sialk. Iron II period, *c.* 1000–800BC. Ht 19.4 cm.

23 (*Left*) View of Burnt Building II at Hasanlu, with restored column bases and hearths and benches along the walls. This building is sometimes identified as a temple.

24 Selection of bronze ingots from a collection found by Sir Aurel Stein at Hasanlu. They were packed into a pottery vessel that was red in colour and partly burnished. The ingots are of two types: bars rounded on one side and flat on the other, and rectangular plates. The discovery of stone moulds in the vicinity, including one for making bar-shaped ingots, shows that metal-working was taking place on the site. Probably 8th–7th century BC. Maximum L (of bars) 27.1 cm, (of plates) 30.5 cm.

gration resulted from an Urartian attack in about 800BC.

A wealth of material was found in the debris of Hasanlu IV. This included glazed wall tiles; iron weapons; seals; an assortment of pottery vessels; 'lion bowls' in ivory, stone and 'Egyptian Blue' (a quartz compound); bronze helmets, bronze vessels and elaborate vessel handles; animal-headed drinking-cups in bronze and Egyptian Blue; pins with iron shanks and bronze lion-heads; and large quantities of horse harness, the most remarkable piece being a bronze horse's breastplate showing, in high relief, a helmeted warrior flanked by two bulls. There were also quantities of furniture, all in fragmentary condition, that had been decorated with bronze, ivory and carved wood.

Particularly outstanding were a gold bowl and a silver beaker. The bowl is covered with scenes of extraordinary interest, probably episodes in some great epic story; amongst the figures depicted are three gods riding in chariots, and a fantastic form which has been identified as a mountain monster. The latter is doing battle with a hero. Found with the bowl in the destruction debris were the skeletons of three men, one of whom had been attempting to carry the bowl to safety when he was overtaken by the sudden collapse of the building. The silver beaker shows in its upper register what is apparently a victory scene, with a prisoner being forced to walk behind a chariot; the figures are slightly raised and covered with an overlay of gold or electrum (an alloy of gold and silver).

These objects from Hasanlu show an artistic style that is clearly local in origin, but there is also evidence of north Syrian and Assyrian influence. Whether the north Syrian influence reached Hasanlu through Assyria or by some independent channel is unknown, but Assyrian influence – most obvious in some of the ivories and seals – is easily explained by geographical proximity and Assyrian interest in the Zagros area.

This Assyrian influence in western Iran became more marked in the ensuing Iron III period. This is hardly surprising: many of the Assyrian kings campaigned there. They may even have approached modern Tehran, if the Mount Bikni of the texts is correctly identified as Mount Demavend, the tallest peak of the Elburz range. Traces of the Assyrian presence in Iran are shown by a few stelae, either freestanding or engraved on rock faces, found in the provinces of Luristan, Hamadan and Kurdistan. These date from the reigns of Sargon (721–705BC), and possibly Tiglath Pileser III (744–727BC) and Ashurbanipal (668–627BC). Actual Assyrian artefacts are more difficult to identify, but a number of bronzes, clearly Assyrian in style, have appeared on the art market in recent years purporting to come from western Iran. This problem of unprovenanced material bedevils much of Iranian ar-

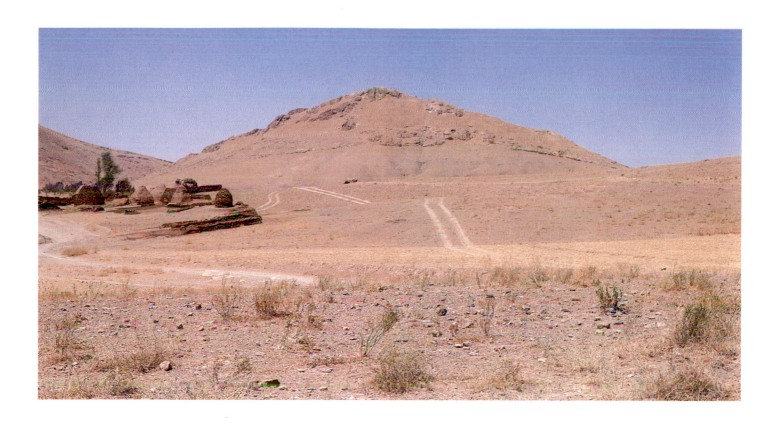

25 View of the high mountain on which the fortified site of Ziwiyeh is situated. Approach to the citadel is by a monumental staircase cut out of the rock that winds round the mountain.

chaeology, but nowhere is this more the case than with Ziwiyeh, one of the best-known sites of the Iron III period.

The site of Ziwiyeh is in Kurdistan, some 40 km from Saqqiz. It occupies a commanding position on top of a prominent hill, surrounded by a massive fortification wall still preserved to a great height in places. The citadel is approached by a monumental staircase cut out of the rock. Ziwiyeh has become notorious for the scale of clandestine excavation and the large number of objects, now scattered in museums around the world, alleged to have come from here. The evidence associating these objects with Ziwiyeh is often vague, if not altogether non-existent, and there is also the possibility that some of the pieces might be faked. The looting of this site first occurred in

about 1946, when local shepherd boys are supposed to have discovered by chance some gold objects, which drew local villagers and antiquities dealers to the site. Initially a bronze coffin of Assyrian type was allegedly found, with chased decoration on the ledge around the top showing processions of human figures. Inside the coffin is thought to have been a rich collection of grave-goods.

Among objects allegedly from Ziwiyeh and now in the Archaeological Museum in Tehran are carved ivories and a magnificent crescent-shaped gold breastplate showing mythical beasts and partly human winged figures. Objects now in the British Museum allegedly from Ziwiyeh include a large fragment of sheet gold, decorated with recumbent stags and ibexes set between interlinked lions' heads;

26 Fragment of gold sheet, c.8th–7th century BC, with perforated border. Allegedly from Ziwiyeh. The recumbent stags and goats are set in panels that incorporate lions' masks. 15.6 × 8.6 cm.

27 strips of gold with lions in the centre and heads of birds of prey along the edge, all executed in a stylised manner in the so-called 'animal art' style associated with south Russia and the Scythians; and a silver frontlet for a horse.

Various theories have been put forward to explain the treasure associated with Ziwiyeh. For example, scholars have suggested that it comes from the tomb of a Scythian prince, or from the burial of a Median chieftain. However, Ziwiyeh was most probably a stronghold of the Manneans, an indigenous Zagros people the centre of whose kingdom lay to the south-east of Lake Urmia. Sandwiched as they were between Urartu to the north, Assyria to the west and the Indo-European groups to the east, their art would surely have reflected influences from these areas combined with a strong local tradition. But we still do not know enough about Ziwiyeh, or indeed about the art of the Manneans in general, to be able to generalise.

However, since the worst ravages of the plunderers there has been some proper excavation – by the Hasanlu expedition in 1964 and, in the late 1970s, by the Iranian archaeologist Nosratollah Motamedi. Finds from the excavations on the citadel and in a cemetery close to the modern village included large numbers of iron leaf-shaped arrowheads; a few bronze socketed arrowheads; part of a bowl with a bird's head on the rim in Egyptian Blue; ivories showing a figure in Assyrian style and a long strip with two lions represented in the so-called 'animal style'; a few seals including two with crude renderings of archers and hunting scenes; and a silver strip decorated with pomegranates.

27 (*Right*) Strips of gold of unknown purpose, allegedly from Ziwiyeh in Kurdistan. The style of the animals and the birds' heads along the edge are thought to be indicative of Scythian or south Russian influence. *c.*8th–7th century BC. L 10.1 cm and 19.4 cm.

28 (*Below*) The modern village of Ziwiyeh seen from the ancient citadel with the mountains of Kurdistan in the background. Some graves in an ancient cemetery behind the village were excavated by an Iranian expedition in the late 1970s.

5 Bronzes of Luristan

Probably the best-known products of the craftsmen of ancient Persia are the so-called Luristan bronzes. These can be found, often in large numbers, in many museums and private collections throughout the world. The British Museum collection alone includes about 175 bronzes that have been catalogued as coming from Luristan. The bronzes are distinctive, attractive, and until recently were modestly priced, making them great favourites with collectors. They have been appearing on the market in quantity since the late 1920s, both in the bazaars of Iran and in the salerooms and dealers' shops of Western Europe and North America. A few bronzes did find their way into collections before this – the British Museum acquired its first example as early as 1854 – but these are exceptional, and the flood did not begin until after 1930. Considering this wealth of material, then, we ought to know a great deal about the bronzes and their background, but sadly this is not the case. Practically without exception these bronzes have been dug up by dealers or local tribesmen; ancient cemeteries and shrines have been systematically looted, and information about the contexts from which the material comes – essential for a proper interpretation – has been irretrievably lost.

What are Luristan bronzes? Some of the objects considered to be of Luristan type are not distinctive of Luristan alone, but have also been recorded in areas such as Elam and Mesopotamia. These cannot be regarded, then, as canonical Luristan bronzes – that is, objects that are characteristic products of the Luristan industry and were not being produced at the same time elsewhere. But even leaving aside these bronzes, there is still a wide range of

29 (*Left*) Bronze horse-bit of Luristan type, with cheek-pieces cast in the form of a master of animals struggling with a grotesque double-headed monster. 10th–7th century BC. W 10.0 cm.

31 (*Above*) Bronze harness-ring with the head of a moufflon and two predatory animals, probably stylised lions, on the sides: a recurrent combination in Luristan art. 10th–7th century BC. 8.8 × 7.0 cm.

30 (*Left*) Bronze horse-bit of Luristan type, with cheek-pieces showing a composite monster with an animal's body, wings, and a horned human head with curling sidelocks. 10th–7th century BC. W 17.1 cm.

material peculiar to Luristan, much of it sharing common features.

The most familiar of the canonical Luristan bronzes are probably horse trappings and harness ornaments. The cheek-pieces that fit on either side of the horse-bits are often very elaborate, sometimes in the shape of ordinary animals such as horses or goats but also in the form of imaginary beasts like winged, human-faced bulls. Other cheek-pieces are bar-shaped, with the ends sometimes cast in the shape of animals' heads, or rectangular with an animal's head at the front top corner. Harness-rings were also popular; these seem to have had a largely decorative function. Typically, they have a ring in the centre which is surmounted by the head of a goat or moufflon; mounted on either side of the central ring, and touching the horns of the moufflon, are two beasts that are probably meant to be lions.

Perhaps the most extraordinary of the Luristan bronzes are the standards or finials, mounted on bottle-shaped cylinders. Many of these standards show the so-called 'master of animals', a Janus-headed human-like figure, in the centre grappling with two beasts. These beasts have long necks and are often leonine. Sometimes the master of animals is not present, and just the two opposing beasts are shown. Often the standards are embellished with the addition of two more heads, either of animals or birds, in the middle. The purpose of these standards is unknown, but it has been suggested that they may have been cult sym-

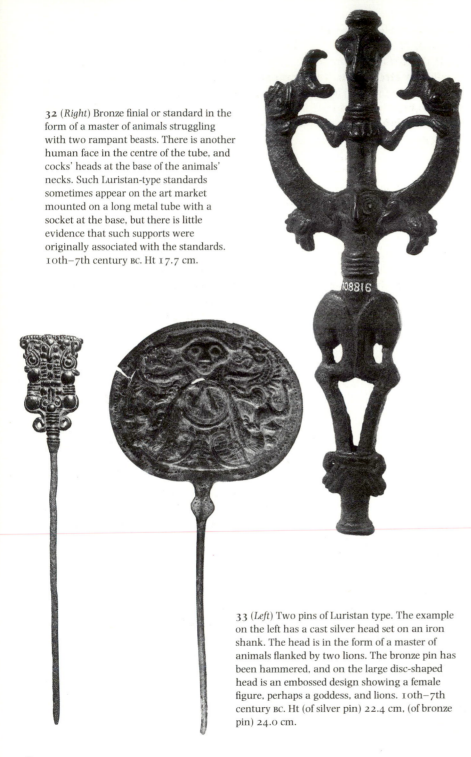

32 (*Right*) Bronze finial or standard in the form of a master of animals struggling with two rampant beasts. There is another human face in the centre of the tube, and cocks' heads at the base of the animals' necks. Such Luristan-type standards sometimes appear on the art market mounted on a long metal tube with a socket at the base, but there is little evidence that such supports were originally associated with the standards. 10th–7th century BC. Ht 17.7 cm.

33 (*Left*) Two pins of Luristan type. The example on the left has a cast silver head set on an iron shank. The head is in the form of a master of animals flanked by two lions. The bronze pin has been hammered, and on the large disc-shaped head is an embossed design showing a female figure, perhaps a goddess, and lions. 10th–7th century BC. Ht (of silver pin) 22.4 cm, (of bronze pin) 24.0 cm.

bols of some sort, perhaps for use in household shrines. Related to the standards are a series of bronze tubes, many in human or partly human form.

Particularly common amongst collections of Luristan bronzes are pins, which occur in a variety of forms. With the more elaborate types the massive heads are always of cast bronze, but the shanks may be of bronze or iron. The heads of these pins may be in openwork or they may be solid; in the range of designs they are comparable to the standards, often featuring the master of animals, but here there is more variation. Sometimes the scenes are highly stylised, and in some cases just a single mythical monster is shown. Other pins have large disc-shaped heads of hammered bronze, again with an interesting range of decorative themes.

The tools and weapons from Luristan are less easy to identify, but some distinctive types may be singled out. For example, there are spike-butted axes in which the spikes terminate in animals' heads, and crescent-shaped axes with a lion's head at the junction between socket and blade. Also characteristic of Luristan are the whetstone handles which often terminate in a goat's head, sometimes with the addition of a lion on the side of the socket.

These various products of the Luristan bronzesmiths all share common features. Animals are the dominant motif, sometimes real but equally often fabulous creatures incorporating wings and occasionally human features. The master of animals is a recurring theme, and goats and lions were particularly popular. The animals show a curious mixture of naturalism and stylisation: the lions especially tend to be stereotyped, with round bulbous eyes, prominent ears, elongated bodies and long tails with a curl at the end. But for the tails and the aggressive pose, they could easily be mistaken for rabbits. There is some variation in the human figures, but they often have

large beaky noses, protuberant eyes and ears that are simply an extension of the face.

A major problem with Luristan bronzes is the large number of fakes in circulation. In addition to crude copies that are fairly easy to identify, there are more sophisticated reproductions posing far greater difficulties. For example, there are after-casts, pieces that are exact replicas of supposedly genuine originals. Sometimes these elaborate forgeries can only be unmasked through detailed analysis and metallographic examination in a laboratory, but even this sort of rigorous inspection is not necessarily foolproof.

The area from which the bronzes are believed to come is in the west central part of Iran, bordered on the west by the high Zagros range that separates Iraq from Iran and extending in the east to Nahavand and Burujird. To the north the area is bounded by the east–west highway, part of the Great Khorasan Road, between Qasr-i Shirin and Kermanshah, and in the south by a line stretching approximately from Mehran to Khorramabad. This region is mountainous, intersected by many

34 (*Above left*) A whetstone for sharpening tools and weapons, with a bronze handle. 10th–7th century BC. L 18.1 cm.

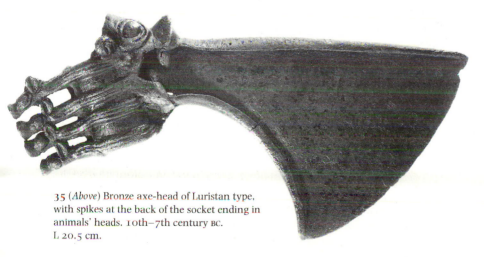

35 (*Above*) Bronze axe-head of Luristan type, with spikes at the back of the socket ending in animals' heads. 10th–7th century BC. L 20.5 cm.

ranges running in a NW–SE direction. But between these mountain ranges are well-watered plains, ideal for breeding horses. In antiquity, access to the region was difficult, and it must have been fairly remote and cut off from outside influences. In fact this is still the case today, which explains why the native inhabitants, the Lurs, have been able to maintain their own dialect and traditions. 38

What do we know of this area in antiquity, and of the society that was producing the bronzes? How are they dated? Why were the bronzesmiths so prolific, and from where did they get their raw materials in such large quantities? These questions cannot yet be satisfactorily answered, mainly because of the relatively small amount of scientific excavation so far undertaken in Luristan. However, there have been a few archaeological expeditions which have contributed greatly to our knowledge of ancient Luristan. Outstanding among these is the work of Professor Louis Vanden Berghe of the University of Ghent, who in the course of fifteen campaigns in the Pusht-i Kuh in western Luristan has excavated at a number of ancient cemeteries. For the Iron Age, these include War Kabud, Tattulban, Bard-i Bal and Chamzhi Mumah. Excavations were also undertaken at the sanctuary site of Dum Surkh by E. Schmidt in 1938, and at Baba Jan by Clare Goff. Both Dum Surkh and Baba Jan are in the Pish-i Kuh in eastern Luristan.

Partly through the results of these excavations, and partly through stylistic considerations and comparison with material from well-dated contexts outside Luristan such as Assyria and the island of Samos, it is clear that the distinctive bronzes of Luristan were being produced between about 1000 and 650BC. Yet it remains a depressing fact that the number of canonical Luristan bronzes from controlled excavations is small, and not all of these have yet been published. In a recent article,

O. W. Muscarella observed that we 'have available for meaningful research less than fifty provenienced artifacts'. Therefore, any sweeping conclusions about the nature of the society in ancient Luristan are best avoided. However, it is striking that many of the Luristan bronzes are horse trappings, suggesting that horsemanship was an important element in the life of ancient Luristan.

It is known that the dead were buried in cemeteries where the graves were often lined on all four sides with stone slabs set upright, and the roof was formed by similar slabs laid flat. This method of construction has supposedly made the graves easy to locate, for archaeologists and grave-robbers alike, as tapping on the surface of the ground is said to produce a hollow ring. The grave-goods might include pottery vessels, weapons and personal ornaments. Distinctive bronzes have been found in graves, in a settlement (Baba Jan) and in a sanctuary (Dum Surkh), but it may be significant that while many disc-headed pins and plaques came from Dum Surkh, no standards or items of horse harness were found there. It seems then that the pins had a votive purpose not shared by other types of bronzes.

A type of pottery sometimes associated with the bronzes, although it may not have the same chronological span or even the same geographical distribution, is often called 'genre Luristan'. It is a cream-coloured pottery, with red-painted designs that are usually geometric, and has been found at Baba Jan and Tepe Giyan. The shapes are sometimes elaborate, as in an anthropomorphic vase from Baba Jan. The same colour paint and similar geometric decoration occurs on large, lightly baked clay tiles from Baba Jan.

Although the distinctive Luristan bronzes date from the first millennium BC, it is clear, both from finds in cemeteries and from unprovenanced material ascribed to Luristan, that there was a flourishing bronze-making

36 (*Above*) Tripod vessel acquired by Sir Aurel Stein in the Rumishgan area of southern Luristan. Red paint on a cream-coloured background is typical of the pottery known as 'genre Luristan'. Ht 19.4 cm.

37 (*Left*) Clay tile from the excavations of Dr Clare Goff at Baba Jan in Luristan. 176 of these tiles had fallen on to the floor of a chamber, probably from the ceiling. 41.5 × 47.0 cm.

36

37

industry in Luristan before that time. These earlier bronzes, though, are similar to contemporary material from Elam and Mesopotamia. So what was the catalyst in this marked change, resulting in the bronzesmiths starting to make such highly distinctive products? One explanation is Nebuchadnezzar's invasion of Elam at the end of the twelfth century BC, and the subsequent decline of Susiana, thus freeing Luristan from the Elamite yoke and giving it a chance to develop along independent lines. Assyrian written sources seem to indicate that modern Luristan corresponds, in part at least, to the ancient kingdom of Ellipi, which maintained its independence during the early part of the first millennium BC and was probably peopled by indigenous inhabitants of the Zagros. We know little about them, however, and crucial questions such as what language they spoke and their precise ethnic origins remain unanswered.

It seems most likely, however, that many of the ideas and motifs that characterise the Luristan bronzes have their origins in Iran, and were not a result of outside influences. For example, the master-of-animals standards may be compared with the decoration on the much earlier fragments of a chlorite bowl found at Ur in Mesopotamia but thought to derive from Iran. And many of the composite monsters appearing on the Luristan bronzes can be found in earlier Elamite art. Indeed, these forms may have been traditional in various parts of Iran, and could have been passed on from generation to generation through local crafts such as textiles and woodwork.

38 Luri women and children tending sheep and goats at Sang-i Surakh near Nahavand in Luristan. Many of the inhabitants of Luristan are still semi-nomadic, and horses are an important part of their way of life.

6 The Medes and the Persians

The Medes first appeared on the historical scene in the ninth century BC, when they were mentioned in contemporary Assyrian texts. They were an Indo-European tribe who, like the related people the Persians, had entered western Iran at some earlier and as yet undetermined date. Thereafter they were in frequent conflict with the Assyrians, their powerful neighbours to the west. Herodotus includes an account of the Medes in his *Histories*, in which he provides a great deal of information, but for the early periods of Median history his account is not entirely credible. We are therefore fortunate that an independent record can be found in Assyrian sources, both textual and illustrative. Representations of campaigns against the Medes, notably during the reigns of Tiglath Pileser III (744–727BC) and Sargon (721–705BC), appear on Assyrian reliefs, and Median fortresses are shown with towers and crenellated battlements. From the reign of Esarhaddon (680–669BC) come the vassal treaties, in which the Assyrian king sought to enlist the support of the Medes in ensuring a peaceful succession to the throne of Assyria.

During the early stages of their history the Medes were probably little more than a loose confederation of tribes, but by the seventh century BC they controlled a wide area around their captial at Ecbatana (modern Hamadan), while the subject Persians were settled in Fars. By 612BC the Medes, under their king Cyaxares, were sufficiently powerful to overthrow in alliance with the Babylonians the ailing Assyrian state. The major Assyrian cities, including Nimrud and Nineveh, were sacked.

Subsequent events in Assyria are not completely clear, but from at least *c.*590BC onwards, the Medes were probably the dominant power in northern Iraq. There is some evidence that the Medes settled the Sagartians, a tribe of Iranian nomads, in the district of Erbil, which probably became an important Median centre. Control over the former centre of the great Assyrian empire would have given the Medes a quick and easy route to Turkey, and in the years after the collapse of Assyria much of eastern Anatolia fell under Median control.

This brought the Medes into direct confrontation with the powerful kingdom of Lydia, which had become well established in west and central Anatolia. Five years of warfare, from 590BC onwards, culminated in the famous battle in 585BC that was dramatically interrupted by a solar eclipse. Peace was made, and the frontier between the Medes and the Lydians was established on the river Halys, with the king of Babylon acting as one of the mediators. Median conquests in the east are less easy to document, but it is possible that Median arms were carried at least into Bactria (northern Afghanistan) and perhaps as far as the river Oxus (Amu Darya). Thus, in the first half of the sixth century BC, the Medes may have loosely controlled a vast tract of territory stretching from the Halys to the Oxus.

It might be assumed that, with this increase in political power and wealth, a distinctive artistic court style would have developed, but traces of the art and material culture of the Medes remain elusive even though in the past many splendid objects have been claimed as Median. These include some of the gold objects in the Oxus Treasure (see chapter 7), as well as swords with gold handles and scabbards: one from a kurgan (burial mound) at Kelermes in the Caucasus, and another in the Melgunov Treasure, found in the Litoy kurgan to the north of the Black Sea. These are decorated with scenes showing winged human figures on either side of a sacred tree, and composite monsters that combine the elements of lions,

39 View of the Median site of Nush-i Jan. The four principal buildings are situated on top of this natural rock outcrop. After this photograph was taken (in 1973), a galvanised iron structure was erected over the Central Temple to protect it from the weather.

bulls, birds of prey and scorpions. There are also recumbent stags on the scabbards. It has been claimed that these swords are Median because they combine Urartian and Scythian artistic elements (which in combination were erroneously supposed to characterise the art of the Medes) and because they are in the form of the Persian *akinakes*, a type of short sword worn by figures in 'Median' dress at Persepolis. A gold-handled sword from Chertomlyk, just to the west of the river Dnieper, has also been called Median because on the handle is a hunting scene comparable with that on the Oxus Treasure scabbard, and at the top of the handle are bulls' heads thought – probably wrongly – to be Urartian in style. There are in addition unprovenanced objects in museums around the world that have from time to time been labelled Median. There is not the slightest evidence, however, for regarding any of these things as Median products or indeed for associating them with the Medes at all.

Given that none of this material is Median, where should we look for evidence of the Medes? Our investigation should begin in the Median heartland, an area bounded by Hamadan, Malayer and Kangavar that has been called 'the Median triangle'. Apart from Hamadan itself, only two major sites in this area which were occupied during the appropriate period – that is, Iron III (c.800–550BC) – have yet been excavated. These are Godin Tepe and Tepe Nush-i Jan. At the former site, excavated by T. Cuyler Young of the Royal Ontario Museum, a series of buildings was found, dating from the Iron III period, which are thought to be part of the residence of a local ruler. The complex includes three columned halls, and at one end is a structure with two series of narrow storerooms and magazines, reminiscent of the so-called 'fort' at Nush-i Jan. Unfortunately, though, apart

39

40 Part of a hoard of silver currency from Tepe Nush-i Jan including quadruple spiral beads, a double spiral pendant (bottom row centre), ingots, rings and scraps of silver. Although the hoard was probably buried in the late 6th century BC, some of the items are very much older, the spiral beads and pendant probably dating from the end of the 3rd or beginning of the 2nd millennium BC. Ht (of pendant) 2.32 cm.

39

from pottery, no small finds of any significance were recovered from this Level II settlement at Godin.

What, then, of Nush-i Jan, the most important Median site yet excavated (by David Stronach, on behalf of the British Institute of Persian Studies, between 1967 and 1977)? Here, on a relatively small mound formed by a natural outcrop of rock, are just four principal buildings: two temples, a columned hall and a fortified structure. The building of this complex probably started around 750BC. The Central Temple has a triangular sanctuary with stepped sides, and it accommodated a mud-brick altar with a shallow depression in the top for holding a fire or burning offerings.

After it fell into disuse this temple was, for some unknown reason, filled with shale chippings to a height of 6 metres and then capped with mud-bricks. The columned hall is a rectangular building with recessed niches on the inside of the walls; the roof was originally supported by twelve wooden columns resting on flat stones. As there are also columned halls at Godin Tepe, these may be a distinctive feature of Median architecture. They can be traced back either to the rectangular columned halls of Level IV at Hasanlu (c.1000–800BC) or perhaps to Urartian columned halls. Although the two temples at Nush-i Jan were closed up and then abandoned, probably between 650 and 600BC, Median occupation continued at the site, principally in the Columned Hall, perhaps as late as 550BC.

The pottery at Nush-i Jan and Godin Tepe – which is presumably typically Median pottery of the seventh and sixth centuries BC, at least from the Hamadan area – is distinctive and belongs to a local tradition. Amongst the most familiar types are bowls with two horizontal handles and jars with vertical handles; this pottery is usually burnished and is reddish-brown or off-white in appearance. Median pottery can thus be identified, but there are difficulties with other types of artefact. The most important find at Nush-i Jan was a silver hoard consisting of bar-ingots, chopped-up pieces of silver, double- and quadruple-spiral beads or pendants, finger-rings, spiral rings, beads, an earring and a bracelet, all packed into a bronze bowl and buried in the floor. It seems clear that this is a hoard of silver currency, the items kept for their intrinsic value rather than for any other purpose. But although this hoard was probably hidden in the sixth century BC, some of the jewellery was of great antiquity even then. The double-spiral pendants and the quadruple-spiral beads seem to date, on the basis of comparisons with other sites, from the end of the third or the beginning of the second millennium BC. Thus this silver hoard tells us little about the material culture of Nush-i Jan in the Median period.

Many of the other finds from Nush-i Jan such as tools, weapons, beads and fibulae are of the sort that can be found at many Middle Eastern sites at this time and are therefore not distinctive of any particular culture. Exceptions are a bronze head of Pazuzu, a Mesopotamian demon; a couple of seals; and a seal impression. This material was current in the Assyrian empire, but whether it was all imported or some at least of the pieces are local copies, is uncertain. The second interpretation is more likely, but in either case there does seem to be some Assyrian influence in the

material culture of the Medes – scarcely surprising in view of the close contacts that existed between Assyria and the Medes, both before and after the collapse of the Assyrian empire. After all, the Medes had ample opportunity to inspect the glories of Assyrian civilisation, and after the destruction of the Assyrian cities they probably brought much booty back to their homeland. This is not to say that this Assyrian or Assyrianising material is illustrative of Median art, which it is not. However, distinctively Median objects *must* have existed. Possibly the Medes had a rich repertoire of luxury items in wood, leather, textiles and so on, but none has survived. It is to be hoped that future excavations at sites such as Hamadan and Erbil will provide much more evidence about the Medes. At Erbil, probably an important administrative centre, there has been no excavation, and we are equally ignorant about their capital city of Hamadan, where there has been a great deal of illicit digging, but this tells us nothing. Recently some proper archaeological excavations have been funded by Hamadan Town Council and organised by the Archaeological Centre in Tehran, but at the time of writing little has been found except traces of a fortification wall that has been described as Median.

This frustrating absence of remains attributable to the Medes is in marked contrast to the situation in the succeeding Achaemenid period, from which we have the magnificent palaces at Persepolis, Pasargadae and Susa. The Achaemenid period may be said to begin in 550BC, when Cyrus the Great deposed the Median king Astyages. Cyrus, who styled himself 'king of Anshan', belonged to the ruling house of Persia but also had Median connections through his mother, whose father was supposedly Astyages, king of the Medes. Cyrus thus established himself as undisputed king of the Medes and the Persians. Amongst his ancestors he counted the legendary king

41 The columned hall of Palace P at Pasargadae. The upper parts of the columns were probably originally made of wood.

Achaemenes, the eponymous founder of the Achaemenid dynasty.

A few years later Croesus, the king of Lydia notorious for his vast wealth, saw an opportunity with the change of regime in Iran to expand his kingdom, and he crossed the river Halys, previously regarded as the boundary between the Lydians and the Medes. Cyrus hastened westwards, and after an inconclusive encounter Croesus retired to his capital city of Sardis. But Cyrus followed him, and in an historic battle defeated the Lydians and captured Sardis in 547 or 546BC. In this way,

much of western Anatolia was brought under his control. Cyrus left his general Harpagus behind to consolidate the Persian position, and shortly afterwards Lycia, Caria and even the Greek cities of Asia Minor were added to his newly founded Persian empire.

About this time Cyrus built himself a capital, in keeping with a king of his status, at Pasargadae – the name may mean 'the Persian settlement' – in Fars. Many early travellers from Europe visited Pasargadae, and excavations have been undertaken by Ernst Herzfeld, Ali Sami and most recently David

42 (*Above right*) Stone relief of Gate R at Pasargadae, showing a four-winged guardian figure wearing an Egyptian crown. Watercolour painted by Sir Robert Ker Porter in 1818. The inscription, in Old Persian, Elamite and Babylonian, reads, 'I, Cyrus, the king, an Achaemenian'. The upper part of the slab is now missing. British Library Add. MS 14758(i) 46/56.

tions in stone of traditional forms in mud-brick and wood. Skilled masons were needed to make the transition from wood to stone, and these Cyrus imported from the newly conquered territories of Ionia and Lydia. The entrance to the gate-house was flanked by winged bulls of Assyrian type, which no longer survive, but a stone relief on one of the doorjambs is still preserved, and this shows a 42 winged genius of Mesopotamian type, wearing an Egyptian crown. These features, combined with Ionian influence in the ashlar masonry of the Tall-i Takht, already show the eclectic nature of Achaemenid art and architecture.

Pasargadae has been described as retaining the character of the settlement of a nomad chief, but this is not altogether true. First, the plan of the settlement is imperfectly known and not altogether comprehensible. Second, the pavilions and their proximity to the palaces, complemented by watercourses, indicate that at least part of the site was laid out as a pleasure park or garden. It was thus the first of the gardens for which Persia has become famous. And third, Pasargadae continued in use – and there was further building work – after the reign of Cyrus, perhaps as a ceremonial or religious centre hosting successive coronations.

Cyrus next turned his attention to his eastern domains: he certainly reached the river Jaxartes (Syr Darya) and may have got as far as the Indus. The time was ripe to add Babylonia to his conquests. Nabonidus, its fanatically religious king, was deposed, and Babylon was captured in 539BC. With it came those parts of the Babylonian empire that had not already defected to Cyrus, and in this way much of Syria and Palestine fell into his hands. Cyrus was now master of an area stretching from the Mediterranean to eastern Iran and from the Black Sea to the borders of Arabia. It was with some justification, then, that in the so-called 'Cyrus Cylinder' – a barrel-shaped

Stronach, on behalf of the British Institute of Persian Studies, from 1961 to 1963. At Pasargadae various structures are spread out across the site, including a gate-house, two small palaces, two pavilions and a large unfinished platform of ashlar masonry (the Tall-i Takht) which was probably the base for a palace that was never built. The palaces have columned halls and porticoes on the sides, and the pavilions are similarly constructed with columns. A solitary column with a stork's nest on top marks the position of one palace.

These buildings were probably reproduc-

41

43 Tomb of Cyrus at Pasargadae, in a watercolour by Sir Robert Ker Porter. British Library Add. MS 14758(i) 47/57.

clay cylinder inscribed in Babylonian cuneiform recording the capture of Babylon – Cyrus described himself as 'ruler of all the world'. Cyrus also relates how he repatriated various peoples and restored the 'images' (of the gods) to their shrines. The Jews are not mentioned by name, but it is clear from the Book of Ezra (I, 1–3) that the captives deported by Nebuchadnezzar were at this time allowed to return to Jerusalem and rebuild the temple.

Cyrus was eventually killed in 530BC while campaigning on his north-east frontier against the Massagetae, somewhere to the east of the Aral Sea. His body was probably brought back to Pasargadae and placed in the structure traditionally called the Tomb of the Mother of Solomon. It is a magnificent stone edifice with a gabled roof, occupying a dominant position set apart from the other buildings at the site. It attracted the attention of many early travellers to the site. Notable amongst them was the famous orientalist Claudius James Rich

who, on visiting the tomb in 1821, wrote: 'The very venerable appearance of this ruin instantly awed me ... I sat for nearly an hour on the steps, contemplating it until the moon rose on it; and I began to think that this in reality must be the tomb of the best, the most illustrious, and the most interesting of Oriental Sovereigns.'

Cambyses (530–522BC), the elder son of Cyrus and his successor, is chiefly remembered for his invasion and subjugation of Egypt and for Herodotus' depiction of him (largely unjustified) as a vicious tyrant, even a madman. The *Histories* of Herodotus, the fifth-century BC Greek historian born at Halicarnassus in Asia Minor, remain the single most important source for the Achaemenid period, but they are supplemented by contemporary Persian and Babylonian sources and by the writings of other classical authors, particularly Ctesias and Xenophon. The revolt at the end of Cambyses' reign is described by Herodotus. It was headed by two *magi*, members of the Median priestly class, one of whom pretended to be Cambyses' murdered brother Bardiya ('the false Smerdis'). On his way from Syria to deal with the revolt, Cambyses was accidentally killed, and the imposter held sway for some months. He was eventually killed by a group of seven conspirators and one of them, Darius, became the next king (522–486BC).

These events are also recorded in Darius' famous relief at Bisitun (Behistun), to the east of Kermanshah on the Great Khorasan Road. High on a cliff-face overlooking the road is a relief showing Darius, accompanied by two attendants, with his foot on the prostrate rebel leader Gaumata. Behind him are nine prisoners, roped together at the neck and hands bound behind their backs. These are kings or chieftains who took advantage of the turmoil caused by Gaumata's rebellion and Darius' usurpation of the throne to throw off the Achaemenid yoke, but within a few years all

44 The rock relief at Bisitun, carved by Darius between 520 and 519BC to commemorate his victories over Gaumata (the false Smerdis) and nine rebel kings from places including Babylonia, Elam, Armenia, Media and Scythia. The kings are shown roped together at the neck, while Gaumata lies under Darius' feet. Above the rebels is a figure in a winged disc, probably the god Ahuramazda. The accompanying inscriptions are written in Old Persian, Elamite and Babylonian, and were copied between 1836 and 1837 by Sir Henry Creswicke Rawlinson. The availability of these texts greatly helped in the decipherment of cuneiform.

were crushed. Above the prisoners is the winged disc containing a human figure, usually thought to represent the god Ahuramazda but sometimes identified as the spirit of the dead king or the divine fortune of the living king. In the accompanying cuneiform inscriptions, written in Old Persian, Babylonian and Elamite, Darius relates how he seized the crown and defeated his various adversaries.

There are further trilingual inscriptions at Ganj Nameh, on one of the slopes of Mount Alvand near Hamadan, and these, together with the Bisitun inscriptions, provided the key for the decipherment of cuneiform. Copies of the texts at Bisitun were first obtained by Sir Henry Creswicke Rawlinson, then a lieutenant in the service of the East India Company, but the Babylonian part of the trilingual inscription gave him great difficulty, as that

part of the relief was on an overhang. An agile Kurdish boy was engaged to climb up the almost vertical rock-face and drive in wooden pegs on either side of the inscription; he fixed a rope between the two pegs and, in Rawlinson's own words, 'with a short ladder he formed a swinging seat, like a painter's cradle, and, fixed upon this seat, he took under my direction the paper cast of the Babylonian inscription.' This was in 1847.

Apart from the expeditions mounted to bring to heel the rebels shown on the Bisitun relief, two campaigns from the early part of Darius' reign stand out. His expedition to India resulted in the annexation of Sind and also possibly the Punjab, but a campaign against the Scythians to the north of the Black Sea was less successful, owing to the mobility and elusiveness of the enemy. Nevertheless, under Darius the Achaemenid empire reached its greatest extent, embracing Egypt and Libya in the west and extending to the river Indus in the east.

To administer this vast empire Darius divided it, according to Herodotus, into twenty provinces, each with its own provincial governor or satrap. Each satrapy was assessed for tax purposes and obliged to provide a fixed annual tribute. In order to make the assessment, more knowledge about the provinces was needed, and this quest for information may have led to the famous voyage of Scylax of Caryanda, who sailed right down the Indus and into the Arabian Sea. Sadly, no record of his discoveries has survived. As an administrator Darius was brilliant, and Herodotus' derisive description of him as a 'tradesman' or 'shopkeeper' does not do him justice. In addition to organising the empire, Darius was the first Persian king to mint coins, and during his reign cuneiform was first used for inscriptions in Old Persian (as at Bisitun). In Egypt he built a canal between the Red Sea and the Nile, anticipating the modern Suez Canal. And it is in Darius' reign that mention is first made of the Royal Road, a great highway stretching all the way from Susa to Sardis with posting stations at regular intervals.

The fact that the road went to Susa was no accident, as this was the most important administrative centre throughout the Achaemenid period and the court probably spent part at least of each year there, as well as at Hamadan. It is a mark of Susa's importance that Darius undertook much building work here; extensive traces have been found in excavations at the site. Most impressive are the Apadana, or audience hall, and an adjoining palace consisting of rooms grouped around large courtyards in the Babylonian tradition. Most of the plan of the Apadana was recovered by Loftus: it consists of a square columned hall with towers at the four corners of the building and, on three sides, porticoes between the towers. The stone columns were very elaborate and supported capitals in the form of two bulls back to back. The Apadana was restored by Artaxerxes II (404–359BC), who also built himself a palace elsewhere on the site at Susa. Traces of other monarchs at Susa include fragments of alabaster vases with trilingual inscriptions of Xerxes, found by Loftus and now in the British Museum.

In the palace that Darius constructed adjoining the Apadana were panels of polychrome glazed bricks, probably decorating courtyard walls. One shows a pair of winged, human-headed lions beneath a winged disc, and another a frieze of royal guards, the so-back cover called 'Immortals'. According to the foundation inscription for the palace, the craftsmen who made and arranged these brick panels came from Babylonia where there was a tradition of this sort of architectural decoration; a particularly well-known example is the Ishtar Gate at Babylon. Other craftsmen employed in the construction of the palace were Ionian and Lydian stonemasons, Median and Egyptian goldsmiths, and Lydian and Egyptian woodworkers.

Also from Susa belonging to the reign of Darius is a headless statue in green schist of the king himself, set on a stone block. This was found in the Gateway of Darius which gave access to the palace enclosure. On the base are representations of his subject peoples, each identified by an inscription in Egyptian hieroglyphs. These, along with the style of the statue and the type of stone, show that it was made in Egypt.

Although Darius founded a number of buildings at Susa, he is better known for his work at Persepolis, the great Achaemenid centre 30 km south-west of Pasargadae, which remains a magnificent memorial to the contents page achievements of the Achaemenid kings. The building programme he initiated was carried on by his two immediate successors, Xerxes

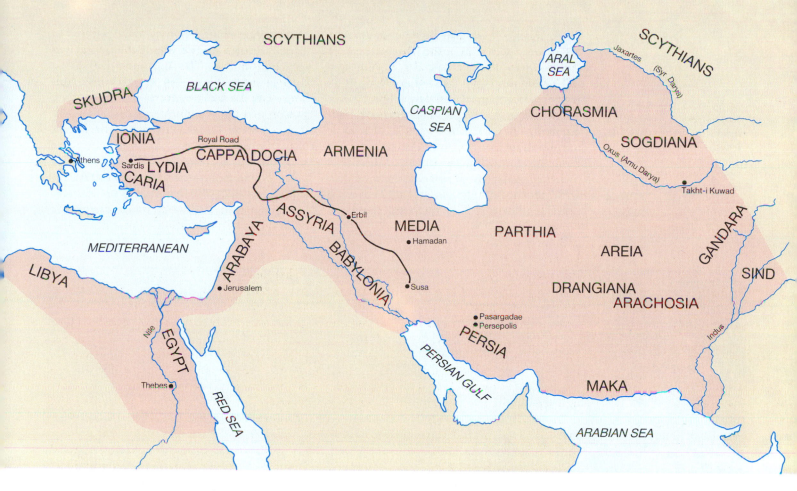

The map shows the Persian Empire with labels including: SCYTHIANS, SKUDRA, BLACK SEA, IONIA, Athens, Sardis, LYDIA, CARIA, Royal Road, CAPPADOCIA, ARMENIA, CASPIAN SEA, ARAL SEA, Jaxartes (Syr Darya), SCYTHIANS, CHORASMIA, SOGDIANA, Oxus (Amu Darya), Takht-i Kuwad, MEDITERRANEAN, ARABAYA, ASSYRIA, Erbil, BABYLONIA, MEDIA, Hamadan, PARTHIA, AREIA, GANDARA, SIND, LIBYA, Jerusalem, Susa, DRANGIANA, ARACHOSIA, Nile, EGYPT, Pasargadae, Persepolis, PERSIA, PERSIAN GULF, Indus, Thebes, RED SEA, MAKA, ARABIAN SEA

45 The Persian empire at the time of Darius (522–486 BC), showing the different satrapies or provinces and the route of the Royal Road from Susa to Sardis.

46

(486–465 BC) and Artaxerxes I (465–424 BC). Darius was buried in a rock-cut tomb at Naqsh-i Rustam, some 6 km north of Persepolis. The façade of the tomb is cut into a cliff and resembles a Greek cross in shape. The central part of the cross is carved to represent the portico of a palace, complete with engaged columns; a door in the centre gives access to the interior of the tomb. Above this palace façade, two rows of bearers, representing the different subject nations of the empire, support a dais on which the king stands before an altar. Above is the figure in the winged disc, possibly Ahuramazda. Also in the same stretch of cliff at Naqsh-i Rustam are three other royal tombs. That of Darius is the only one identified by an inscription, but it is thought that the others may have belonged to Xerxes, Artaxerxes I, and Darius II (423–404 BC).

Towards the end of Darius' reign the much publicised struggle with Greece began, which ended in ignominy for the Persians. The scale and importance of the conflict have probably been much exaggerated, largely because it has become so well known in the West through Herodotus' lengthy and enthralling account. But were it not for Herodotus and other classical sources, we would know almost nothing of this encounter: the written Persian sources are entirely silent on this question.

46 A view of the cliff at Naqsh-i Rustam, showing the tombs of Artaxerxes I (464–424BC) on the left and Darius (522–486BC). In the centre at the base of the cliff is a Sasanian relief showing Shapur I (AD240–72) triumphing over two of his Roman adversaries.

The trouble began when the Ionians in Asia Minor revolted and, with the support of Athens and Eretria, sacked Sardis. Although the revolt was suppressed, Darius seems to have found this interference by Greek states in Asiatic affairs to be quite unacceptable. Consequently, he sent Mardonius with a large army and fleet across into Europe with the intention of attacking Eretria and Athens, but inclement weather at sea and clashes with local tribesmen forced this expedition to withdraw. A still larger force under the command of Artaphernes and Datis was dispatched in 490BC. Eretria on the island of Euboea was captured, and after crossing the Gulf of Euboea the Persian troops landed on the Greek mainland near the Plain of Marathon. There they were confronted by the Athenians under Miltiades, and in the ensuing battle the Greeks clearly gained the upper hand. The Persians were forced to retreat to their ships, but nevertheless still pressed towards Athens by sailing round Cape Sounion. By the time they arrived off Athens, however, the occupants of

the city had already been alerted by the epic run of Pheidippides (thereby immortalising in athletic circles the name of Marathon) and had prepared their defences. The Persians had little choice but to withdraw.

There followed a lull in hostilities until Darius' successor Xerxes renewed the conflict. In the early part of Xerxes' reign there were troubles in Egypt and Babylonia to deal with, and not until his sixth year was he ready to turn his attention towards Greece. After crossing the Hellespont with a large force, he marched unopposed through Thrace, Macedonia and Thessaly but found his way into central Greece blocked at the pass of Thermopylae. The confederate Greek troops occupied a strong position in the narrow pass but, acting on information supplied by a Greek defector, the Persians were able to attack them from behind. When they realised the hopelessness of their position most of the Greek troops withdrew, leaving Leonidas in charge of a small band including 300 Spartans to hold up the Persian advance and cover the Greek retreat. They fought a heroic rearguard action, but it was to no avail.

The way was then clear for Xerxes to advance on Athens and occupy the almost deserted city. On the acropolis temples were looted and burnt, and destruction was widespread. The Athenians meanwhile had withdrawn to Salamis, as had the Greek fleet, to prepare for an expected battle at the Isthmus of Corinth. Xerxes would have to win this in order to gain control of the Peloponnese. The Greek and Persian fleets clashed in the Straits of Salamis, where the Greeks under Themistocles won a convincing victory; many of the Persian ships were destroyed and many of their troops were drowned.

Xerxes had no alternative but to withdraw for the time being, leaving Mardonius behind in northern Greece while he himself returned to Asia. The next year, 479BC, Mardonius again advanced into Attica and then withdrew to the Theban plain. The Greeks abandoned their position on the Isthmus of Corinth and the two armies met on the Plain of Plataea near Thebes. The result was a famous victory for the Greeks commanded by Pausanias of Sparta. Mardonius himself was killed and the Persians were routed. On the same day according to popular tradition, but probably some time later, Greek warriors landed on the coast of Asia Minor near Mount Mycale and defeated the Persian army under Tigranes (part of the large force evacuated from Greece the previous autumn).

The Achaemenid attempt to overrun Greece was thus ended. From the beginning it had been an ill-considered venture: united, the Greek states were a formidable adversary, and for such a large Persian force to advance into Greece required impossibly long lines of communication. The Persians were also fighting with very large numbers of subject peoples in their ranks, and it is doubtful whether their loyalty and enthusiasm could always be counted upon.

In the latter part of his reign Xerxes was preoccupied on the one hand with his building programme at Persepolis and on the other with harem intrigues. These are reflected in the Book of Esther, which describes how Esther (a Jewess) married King Ahasuerus (Xerxes) and was able to prevent a planned massacre of the Jews. Whatever the truth of this, Xerxes was assassinated in his palace in 465BC. Under his successor Artaxerxes I, building work continued at Persepolis and, by the end of his long reign, the plan was more or less complete except for some minor additions and alterations during the reign of Artaxerxes III (359–338BC).

Many early travellers visited Persepolis and have left accounts of the ruins, but our main knowledge of the site derives from an expedition sponsored by the University of Chicago that was in the field from 1931 to 1939, led first by Ernst Herzfeld and then by Erich Schmidt; the results of this work are published in three sumptuous volumes. More recently there has been some further excavation and restoration work, notably that of Giuseppe and Ann Britt Tilia. The most important buildings at Persepolis were crowded on to a terrace of natural rock (Takht-i Jamshid) that rises from the plain on three sides and abuts a low mountain on the fourth side. There are about fifteen major buildings, including the Apadana, the Hall of 100 Columns, the Gate-House of Xerxes, the Treasury, the 'Harem', the so-called Central Building, and the palaces of Darius, Xerxes, Artaxerxes I and Artaxerxes III. The existing remains consist of stone columns with elaborate bases and capitals, stone door- and window-jambs, and façades and staircases, many with relief sculpture. They make Persepolis one of the most impressive sites not just in Iran but in the whole of the ancient world. However, the fact that so much of the stonework is preserved actually gives a misleading impression of how the site would have looked in antiquity, because the original mud-brick walls, an important element of the architecture, have entirely disappeared.

It has been suggested that Persepolis was a ceremonial site, principally used for the No-Ruz (New Year) festival at the time of the spring equinox, but this theory is not altogether convincing. It is true that Persepolis was not as important an administrative capital as Susa, and indeed it was practically ignored by the classical authors. Yet our knowledge of the site as a whole is still limited, making interpretation difficult; we have a detailed knowledge of the terrace platform, or citadel, but know little about the buildings in the surrounding plain where there was an extensive outer town.

The Gate-House of Xerxes on the terrace platform, known as the 'Gate of All Lands', is,

47 (*Left*) Detail of relief from Persepolis showing a Persian archer holding a spear. From the north side of the Apadana, south side of the north-west stairs. Ht c.32 cm.

49 (*Right*) The Gate-House of Xerxes at Persepolis. The entrance is flanked by two massive winged bulls with human heads of Assyrian type.

48 (*Above*) Relief from Persepolis showing file of so-called Susian guards armed with spears. From the north side of the Apadana, east wing, upper register. L 107 cm.

like the gate-house at Pasargadae, decorated with winged, human-headed bulls ultimately of Assyrian origin. The Apadana, on the other hand, finds its closest parallel at Susa: the plans of the two buildings are basically the same, consisting of a square columned hall with towers at the corners and porticoes on three sides. In both cases, the columns support double-bull capitals. Both buildings were founded by Darius.

However, the Apadana at Persepolis is built on a stone platform decorated with staircases and relief sculpture on the north and east 51, 53 sides. Each side is a mirror image of the other, but whereas the north side has been exposed 53 for centuries and is now in poor condition, the east side was only uncovered by the Chicago 51 expedition and is therefore in a much better state of preservation. The reliefs originally showed the enthroned Persian king in the centre (this panel was later replaced), while towards him moved processions of tributaries. Altogether twenty-three different subject peoples are shown, including Medes, Elamites, Babylonians, Lydians, Scythians, Indians, Egyptians, Nubians and Libyans. All are dressed in their national costume and all bring different sorts of presents – intrinsically valuable or exotic objects, or items typical of their region. The Elamites, for example, bring lions and weapons; the Lydians bring bracelets, vessels presumably of precious metal, and a harnessed chariot; and the Medes are carrying 52 clothes, bracelets, a short sword or *akinakes*, and vessels. They are dressed in the distinctive Median costume of knee-length tunic, tight-fitting trousers and cap with ear-flaps and neck-guard. Elsewhere on the Apadana reliefs, a *kandys* (long-sleeved coat) slung over the shoulders is added to the Median costume. This outfit is different from the usual Persian 50 costume of a long pleated dress. Behind the king are attendants and guards, and other soldiers line the stairs and parapets. By careful

50 (*Left*) Nobles in Persian and 'Median' dress, from the east side of the Apadana at Persepolis.

51 (*Left*) Section of the relief on the south wing of the east side of the Apadana at Persepolis, showing (top to bottom) delegations IV (Arians?); V (Babylonians); and VI (Lydians).

53 (*Right*) Persepolis relief showing grooms carrying saddle-cloths and whips. From the north side of the Apadana, east wing. Ht 45.0 cm.

52 (*Right*) Persepolis relief showing a servant, in so-called Median dress, holding a covered goblet. This sculpture dates from the reign of Artaxerxes III, and comes either from Darius' Palace or from Palace G. Ht 75.5 cm.

54 (*Far right*) Stone relief in the Hall of 100 Columns at Persepolis (east jamb of eastern doorway in southern wall), showing an enthroned king supported by people representing different parts of the Persian empire. Photograph of a cast taken from a mould made at Persepolis in 1891.

study of the Apadana reliefs, Michael Roaf has recently demonstrated that they were carved by sculptors working in teams, each of which signed its work with a distinctive mason's mark. There are also reliefs showing attendants in Persian or Median dress and guards in the Central Building and in four of the palaces, while subject peoples also appear in the palaces of Darius and Artaxerxes I. In addition, large reliefs with majestic representations of the king are found on the door-jambs of many of the buildings.

The king is, in fact, an omnipresent and dominant figure in the sculpture at Persepolis, and it seems that the whole purpose of the decorative scheme was to glorify the king, his majesty and his power. In this way the Persepolis sculptures are not quite the same as the Assyrian reliefs, which are essentially narrative and aim to illustrate the achievements of the king. The similarities are such, though, that it is obvious much of the inspiration for this sort of relief decoration must have come from Assyria, and indeed some compositions can be exactly paralleled.

Precisely how this influence was transmitted is unclear; even by the time of Cyrus, the Assyrian cities had lain abandoned for more than half a century. Perhaps some of the sculptures were still visible, or possibly the artistic tradition was passed on by the Medes. Although we have no evidence at all of Median relief sculpture in stone, wooden sculptures are mentioned in texts from Persepolis. But it is not only Assyrian influence that is discernible in Achaemenid sculpture. Greek, Egyptian, Urartian, Babylonian, Elamite and Scythian influences (and others) have all been recognised. This is perhaps not surprising in view of the wide range of workmen who are known to have been employed by the Archaemenid kings in the construction work at Persepolis and its environs. The tablets found in the Treasury and in the Fortification Wall at Persepolis, written in Elamite, mention among others Egyptians, Syrians, Ionians and Babylonians. An indication of the different nationalities used in building works, and their specialities, is given by the foundation inscription of Darius' palace at Susa (p.40). The employment of these various craftsmen is reflected in the creation of a new official art style in keeping with the status of the Achaemenid kings as 'rulers of the world'. Elements were drawn from various cultures and welded together to form an artistic style that was in the end distinctively Achaemenid. This fusion of styles was perhaps the main Persian contribution, but there was also a local ingredient that manifested itself chiefly in the extensive use of columns and in distinctive plans such as the apadana form.

In view of the great size of the Achaemenid empire, any enquiry into the material culture of the period must extend far beyond the borders of modern Iran. This is particularly the case with minor arts and crafts. While there is to some extent a wide variety of styles and forms, there is on the other hand a recognisably Achaemenid style, perhaps promoted outside Iran by satraps and other representatives of the Persian court.

Vessels of precious metal were widespread, and two particularly distinctive forms seem to have been common: the amphora with two animal-shaped handles, and the rhyton (horn-shaped drinking cup) ending in an animal's head. On a more popular level, there are a number of bowls decorated with a lotus flower or a rosette in the centre. The cylinder seals of this period are often immediately recognisable by the winged disc and figures dressed in Persian or Median costume.

Achaemenid jewellery was especially magnificent, as shown by the quality of the pieces found in a hoard at Pasargadae. In particular, the circular open-work earrings with their intricate goldwork are outstanding. Bracelets

55 (*Right*) Bronze figure of a reclining ibex, hollow-cast, with slots on the underside for fixture. Perhaps from an elaborate piece of furniture. Acquired by the British Museum with the aid of the National Art Collections Fund and the Littauer Fund. Achaemenid period, 5th–4th century BC. Ht 29.5 cm.

58 (*Far right*) Silver bowl with applied gold figures on the underside, showing a winged lion with the head of the Egyptian dwarf-god Bes, complete with feather crown. There is a comparable gold bowl in the Oxus Treasure. Achaemenid period, 5th–4th century BC. D 17.2 cm.

56 (*Above*) Agate cylinder seal with modern impression showing a royal lion hunt. The scene is framed by date palms, and a figure in a winged disc, possibly Ahuramazda, hovers above. The chariot may be compared with the gold example in the Oxus Treasure **front cover**. The inscription, in Old Persian, Elamite and Babylonian, records the name of 'Darius the great king', probably Darius I (522–486BC). This seal was reportedly found in Egypt. Ht 3.3 cm.

57 (*Below*) Silver bowl with applied gold decoration, showing battlements at the top and two rows of figures below. Each has a bow and quiver on his back and wears a crown, suggesting a Persian king may be depicted. Achaemenid period, 5th–4th century BC. D 10.3 cm.

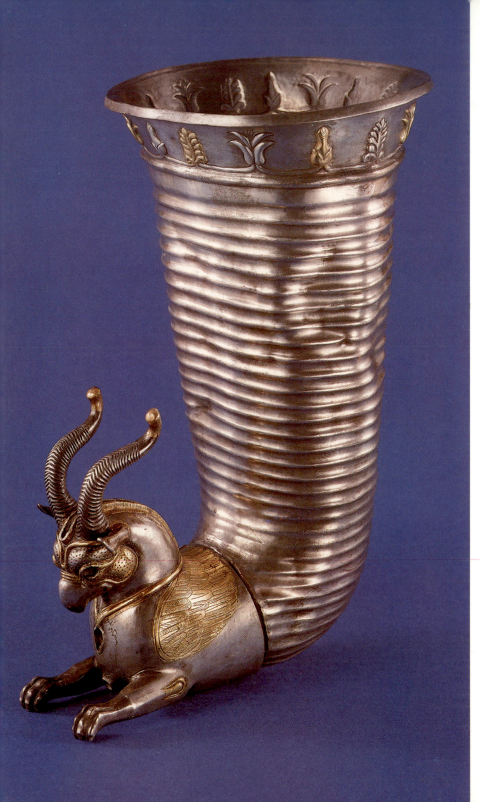

with animal-shaped terminals are another distinctive form. For simple bracelets the terminals are often in the form of goats' heads, but winged griffins were preferred on heavier, more elaborate examples. Other items such as bronze furniture fittings can be identified as Achaemenid through their depiction on the reliefs.

Most of this material, though, falls into the category of what is termed Achaemenid court style; the repertoire of less expensive, utilitarian objects is much less well known. This is because, apart from the major Achaemenid centres in Iran – and one could add to those already described Dahan-i Ghulaman in Sistan – few sites of Achaemenid date have been excavated. Even Achaemenid pottery is poorly known. It is ironic, then, that more is known about the material culture of the Achaemenid period in Syria and Palestine than in Iran and Iraq. A wide range of material including weapons and personal ornaments was recovered from the cemeteries at Deve Hüyük in Syria, and in Palestine more than seventy excavated sites have produced material dated to the Achaemenid period. There is also an important Achaemenid cemetery at Kamid el-Loz in the Lebanon.

After the reign of Artaxerxes I, the Achaemenid empire lost much of the momentum that had characterised its formative years, and there began a long period of decline. One particularly notorious dispute for the throne, recorded by Xenophon in his *Anabasis*, was between Artaxerxes II and Cyrus the Younger, whose army included Xenophon and 10,000 Greek mercenaries. Although there were brief periods of recovery, by the late fourth century BC the time was ripe for Alexander the Great and his Macedonian troops to overthrow the Achaemenid empire.

59 Silver rhyton, reportedly from Erzincan. Achaemenid period, 5th–4th century BC. Ht 25.0 cm.

7 The Oxus Treasure

The collection of gold and silver objects and coins known as the Oxus Treasure is the most important hoard of Achaemenid metal-work yet discovered. It was apparently found in 1877 on the banks of the Oxus (Amu Darya), the great river that flows from the Pamirs to the Aral Sea and in its upper reaches separates the modern state of Afghanistan from the Soviet Union.

The treasure was nearly lost three years later and only recovered by chance in extraordinary, even bizarre circumstances. According to O. M. Dalton, whose 1905 catalogue of the Oxus Treasure remains the basic publication, in May 1880 bandits seized three merchants from Bokhara as they were travelling with the treasure from Kabul to Peshawar. However, their servant was able to escape and raise the alarm in the camp of Captain F. C. Burton, a British political officer in Afghanistan. Burton set off with two orderlies and came across the robbers in a cave shortly before midnight. They were in the process of dividing their spoil and had already been quarrelling over it; four were lying wounded. We are told that 'a parley ensued', as a result of which much of the treasure was given up to Burton. The next day he threatened to lead a force against the robbers, which persuaded them to bring in another large part of the treasure. In this way about three-quarters was restored to the merchants and, as a token of their gratitude, they allowed Burton to purchase the large gold armlet subsequently acquired by the Victoria and Albert Museum.

The merchants continued on their journey to Peshawar and eventually sold the treasure at Rawalpindi. It was gradually acquired from dealers there by Major General Sir Alexander Cunningham, Director General of the Archaeological Survey of India. Cunningham in turn sold the pieces to Sir Augustus Wollaston Franks, who on his death in 1897 bequeathed them to the British Museum.

There is some confusion about the provenance of the Oxus Treasure. Cunningham, who wrote several articles about the treasure, said in his earliest accounts that it had been found near Takht-i Kuwad, a ferry-station on the north bank of the Oxus opposite Khulm (now Tashkurghan), two days' journey from Kunduz. The pieces were scattered about in the sands of the river. In the last article he wrote about the treasure, however, he preferred to regard it as coming from Kabadian (now known as Mikoyanabad or Nasir Khisrav), a large village just under 50 km north of the Oxus, on its tributary the Kafirnigan river. It seems more likely, though, that the treasure was indeed found on the banks of the Oxus, and the Soviet scholar E. V. Zeimal has cited contemporary Russian accounts that seem to support Takht-i Kuwad as the find-spot of the treasure. According to Zeimal, the ruins here occupy a square kilometre, about a quarter of which has been washed away by the river.

Takht-i Kuwad is actually one of two fortresses on the right bank of the Oxus guarding the ferry crossing; the other is Takht-i Sangin, where a Soviet expedition has found a temple with surrounding corridor-storerooms full of valuable objects. Most of this material dates from the Hellenistic period, but a few items, such as a finely decorated ivory scabbard for an *akinakes* or short sword, are of Achaemenid date. Although far from Persepolis, Takht-i Kuwad was still well within the Achaemenid empire. North of the river Oxus, where the treasure was reputedly found, was the satrapy of Sogdia, while to the south was Bactria.

Altogether about 170 items are associated with the Oxus Treasure, the vast majority in gold or silver and mostly dating from the fifth to fourth centuries BC. There are just a few that might be either earlier or of third century BC date or later. To what extent this treasure is a single, discrete find must always, in view of the manner of its discovery, remain a matter of

60 (*Left*) Gold scabbard cover for an *akinakes* or short sword, from the Oxus Treasure. The embossed decoration shows the various stages of a royal lion hunt, for which the inspiration may have been drawn from Assyrian reliefs of the 7th century BC. This is probably the oldest object in the Oxus Treasure. 6th–5th century BC. L 27.6 cm.

speculation. In the absence of any first-hand accounts we can never be sure that all the pieces were found together in a single spot; pieces could also have been added during the journey from Takht-i Kuwad to Rawalpindi, or more likely the dealers in Rawalpindi might have supplemented the treasure with pieces from elsewhere. There is even evidence that some faked pieces were passed off in Rawalpindi as belonging to the treasure, but as far as we know all the pieces now in the British Museum are authentic. In spite of these reservations, though, the Oxus Treasure does have the appearance of a homogeneous group and might well have been found in the circumstances described.

One of the earliest pieces in the treasure, and also one of the most splendid, is a gold scabbard for an *akinakes*. The thin gold, which was originally on another material such as wood or leather, is embossed with scenes showing a lion hunt. These hunting scenes are reminiscent of Assyrian reliefs from the time of Ashurbanipal (668–627BC) and the horsemen, although wearing trousers in the Iranian fashion, have headgear not dissimilar to that worn by Assyrian kings. These Assyrian parallels indicate a relatively early date for the scabbard.

There are many magnificent objects in the

61 (*Above*) Gold plaque from the Oxus Treasure, showing a man dressed in the so-called Median costume of belted tunic and trousers. He wears a soft cap that covers the ears and chin, and has an *akinakes* (short sword) at his side. This figure is sometimes identified as a priest because of the bundle of sticks (barsom) he carries, originally grasses that were distributed during religious ceremonies. 5th–4th century BC. Ht 15.0 cm.

Oxus Treasure, but amongst the best known is
a pair of gold armlets with terminals in the
shape of horned griffins, originally inlaid with
glass and coloured stones. Also in the treasure
are a number of other animal-headed bracelets, in gold and in gold and silver.

The single largest component of the treasure,
however, is a group of nearly fifty thin gold
plaques, ranging in height from under 3 cm to
almost 20 cm; they have chased outlines of
human figures, some very crude and roughly
executed that smack of local or amateur
workmanship. Many of the figures wear
Median dress – a cap with ear-flaps and
neckguard, trousers and a long-sleeved belted
tunic. Sometimes this outfit is accompanied by
an *akinakes*, and a few of the figures wear a
kandys. Several carry barsoms (bundles of
sticks), which has prompted the suggestion
that they, and perhaps others in Median dress,
are priests. Of course, the fact that the figures
are wearing Median dress does not mean that
the plaques date from the Median or pre-
Achaemenid period, because we know that
the Median costume was widespread in
Achaemenid times and later and was not
confined to Medes. We do not really know the
purpose of these plaques, but one possibility is
that they may have been votive plaques
intended for a temple or shrine.

One of the most outstanding pieces in the
treasure is a model chariot pulled by four
horses or ponies; in the chariot are a driver and
seated passenger, both again wearing Median
dress, as are two free-standing small gold
statuettes. Another much larger figure in
silver is of a nude youth; he wears a Persian
head-dress, but his nudity indicates Greek
influence. A large gold head of a boy is bare-
headed, but Greek influence here is less obvious and this could be a local product. The
vessels in the treasure include a hemispherical
gold cup; a silver bowl with rosette in the
centre and radiating petals; a gold jug with

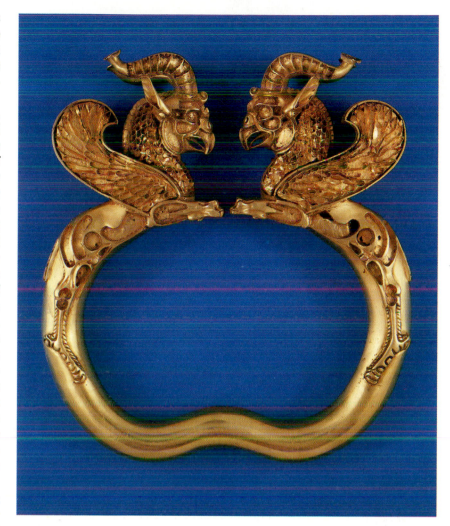

62 (*Above*) Massive gold bracelet from the Oxus Treasure, with terminals in the form of
winged griffins. Originally inlaid with glass and coloured stones. Large animal-headed
bracelets are shown being presented to the king by four of the delegations on the Apadana
reliefs at Persepolis. Xenephon tells us in the *Anabasis* that armlets were among the items
considered gifts of honour at the Persian court. 5th–4th century BC. W 11.5 cm.

handle ending in a lion's mask; a gold om-phalos bowl with a frieze of embossed lions on the underside; and a cast silver vessel-handle in the form of a springing ibex. There are also circular gold plaques, perhaps clothing or-naments; a few cylinder seals; and a number of signet-rings with engraved designs on the bezel.

In addition, about 1500 coins were orig-inally associated with the treasure. Like the objects, they were sold off in Rawalpindi and were said to belong to the treasure. Some scholars have been reluctant to accept the coins as an integral part of the hoard, but it is illogical, when all are said to have been found together, to reject the coins and accept the objects as a single collection. Some of the coins were acquired by Cunningham, some were bought by Mr A. Grant, Chief Engineer and Director of the Indian Railways, and others were randomly dispersed. The largest col-lection is now in the British Museum, and a small number are in the State Hermitage in Leningrad.

Many of the items in the Oxus Treasure are representative of what we have called Ach-aemenid court style, a formal style found throughout the empire and considered typical of the Achaemenid period. But there are also other elements. Some Greek influence has already been noted, and a few provincial products can be singled out, including a silver statuette of a man wearing a head-dress and 64 pleated costume that are apparently copies of standard Persian types of dress.

What exactly was the Oxus Treasure? Most likely it was a hoard of currency – there is a long tradition in the ancient Middle East of using precious metal, gold and particularly silver, for the purposes of exchange. The metal had a purchasing power equivalent to its weight, and continued to be used for currency even after the introduction of coinage. There is evidence of this practice in the Persepolis

64 (*Above*) Silver statuette, partially gilded, probably of a king. From the Oxus Treasure. 5th–4th century BC. Ht 14.8 cm.

63 (*Left*) Cast silver statuette with gilding on the Persian style head-dress, from the Oxus Treasure. 5th–4th century BC. Ht 29.2 cm.

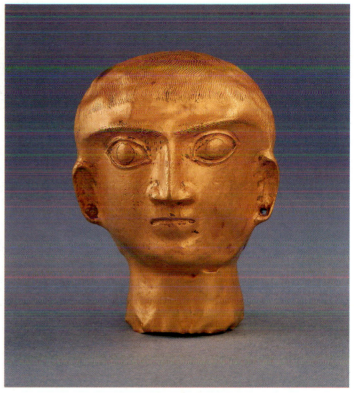

65 (*Above left*) Gold jug from the Oxus Treasure, with lion-headed handle. 5th–4th century BC. Ht 13.0 cm.

66 (*Above right*) Gold head of a beardless youth with pierced ears, from the Oxus Treasure. This was presumably part of a statue, perhaps made of another material such as wood. 5th–4th century BC. Ht 11.3 cm.

tablets, dating from the first half of the fifth century BC, in which payments are expressed in amounts of silver. The character of the Oxus Treasure, consisting partly of a collection of gold and silver objects, some of them mutilated, and partly of a large number of coins, is consistent with its identification as a hoard. Other near-contemporary hoards are the silver hoard from Nush-i Jan (p.35) and the Chaman-i Hazuri hoard from Kabul, consisting of bent bar silver coins and standard Greek and Achaemenid issues, which was probably buried in the mid-fourth century BC.

Assuming that it was indeed a hoard, when was the Oxus Treasure buried? Here, numismatic evidence is invaluable. The coins range in date from the early fifth century to the early second century BC, and include mainland Greek, Achaemenid and Hellenistic issues. Zeimal has suggested that the very latest coins are different in character from the rest, and were probably added in Rawalpindi. He believes that the latest coins definitely associated with the Treasure are from the reign of Euthydemus I of Bactria (*c.*235–200BC). This might indicate, then, that the Oxus Treasure was buried towards the end of the third century BC, but we still do not know who concealed it or why, or under what circumstances it was originally collected.

8 From Alexander to Islam

In 334BC a sequence of events began that had a profound influence on the whole of western Asia. In that year, Alexander the Great with his Macedonian army crossed the Hellespont, and the Persian armies of Darius III were defeated first at the river Granicus, then at Issus, and finally at Gaugamela in northern Iraq in 331BC. These defeats are vividly commemorated in a mosaic at Pompeii and on the so-called Alexander sarcophagus from Sidon, now in Istanbul. The way was now open for Alexander to march into Iran itself and, once there, he committed a supreme act of vandalism. Having looted Susa, he turned towards Persepolis, and that magnificent complex of buildings was put to the torch. Whether it was an act of drunken folly or revenge for Xerxes' destruction of the acropolis at Athens, it was surprising behaviour from one who prided himself on being a pupil of Aristotle.

Within a few years, Alexander went on to overrun the rest of Iran and the eastern provinces of the Persian empire. After Alexander's death in 323BC, however, his generals quarrelled over the division of his empire. In the east Seleucus emerged victorious, and by 300BC he was in control not only of Iran but also of Mesopotamia and north Syria. Hellenistic control of Iran lasted in all for about a century and a half.

During the Hellenistic period, the Achaemenid administrative division of the empire into satrapies was retained. Initially Alexander's policy was to appoint native Iranians as satraps or governors in Iran and further east, supported by Greco-Macedonian generals who probably wielded the real power. It is sometimes argued that Alexander's intention was to create a mixed Greco-Iranian ruling class; at one great banquet at Susa he actually ordered his officers to take Persian wives. However, even before the end of Alexander's life most of the Iranian satraps had been replaced by Macedonians and – with the exception of places such as Susa – the extent to which Macedonians and Persian integrated has probably been exaggerated.

Hellenistic policy was to establish military colonies and cities (*poleis*) on the main trade routes and at other strategic positions. Thus during this period we see the foundation (or refoundation) of Susa (Seleucia on the Eulaios), Hamadan (Epiphaneia), Rayy (Europos) and Shahr-i Qumis (Hecatompylos). The Seleucid interest in trade and commerce dictated the foundation of cities around the Persian Gulf such as Ikaros (on the island of Failaka), Spasinou Charax (now in Iraq), and Antiocha (probably near Bushir). Overall control was maintained from the eastern Seleucid capital at Seleucia on the Tigris in Mesopotamia. Macedonian settlers probably lived in these Greek centres rather than in the countryside, but Iranians could if they chose become citizens of a Greek *polis* in Iran.

Limited evidence is available concerning the extent of Greek influence on Iran. Certainly the Greek language was widespread at this time – although Aramaic continued to be used as a written language – but this could have been a result of Greek control of the major urban centres, which were the strongholds of literacy. Away from these centres, Hellenistic influence may have been much less.

For Iran as a whole, the sources are meagre and significant finds are few and far between. These include part of a large bronze head from the sanctuary at Shami in Elam, which has been identified as that of a Seleucid king, possibly Antiochus IV; the statue of a reclining Heracles at Bisitun, dated by an inscription to 148BC; and a Greek inscription on stone from Nahavand, probably from a temple, recording the establishment by Antiochus III of a cult for his wife Laodicea in 193BC. The famous stone lion of Hamadan, unfortunately much battered over the passage of time, is probably also a Hellenistic monument, perhaps carved at the order of Alexander to commemorate his general Hephaestion, who died in Hamadan. In the absence of inscriptions the foundation dates of temples are often controversial, but most authorities agree that the two surviving columns with Ionic capitals at Khurheh, about halfway between Tehran and Isfahan, date from the Hellenistic period, although they are of local workmanship. Hellenistic pottery is more widespread than identifiable Hellenistic monuments, occurring on sites such as Persepolis and Pasargadae, but many more surveys need to be done.

Hellenistic influence was particularly strong at Susa, continuing well into the Parthian period. Susa became a proper Greek *polis* with a Greek civic organisation, gymnasiums, theatres and so on. Even Greek gods were worshipped in the city, as we know from coins and inscriptions found there. Not surprisingly, numerous traces of Hellenistic occupation have been found by French archaeologists as well as by Loftus, who discovered secondary Greek inscriptions cut on to Achaemenid column bases and fragments of an alabaster statuette showing a woman dressed in the Greek style.

The first serious challenge to Seleucid control of Iran came in about 238BC, when the Parthians seized control of the satrapy of Parthia, situated east of the Caspian Sea. In origin they were a nomadic Iranian tribe who migrated into the area from central Asia. Arsaces, founder of the dynasty, and his immediate successors spent the succeeding years establishing themselves and expanding at the expense of the Seleucids. Their two most important early capitals were at Nysa (ancient Mithradatkirt), now in Soviet Turkmenistan, and Shahr-i Qumis (ancient Hecatompylos) near Damghan. This Parthian expansion was not without its setbacks, but by 141BC Mithradates I, who is often regarded as the real founder of the Parthian empire, was in a

position to be crowned at Seleucia-on-the-Tigris in Mesopotamia. Perhaps at this time a winter capital was established at Ctesiphon on the opposite bank of the river. At the time of his death, in about 138BC, the Parthians were in control of much of the Iranian plateau and Mesopotamia and part of central Asia. In spite of some further reverses, by 113BC his successor Mithradates II had extended the western frontier of the Parthian empire to the Euphrates.

By now Parthia was firmly straddling the Silk Route, greatly benefiting from its role as a middleman in the exchange of goods between China in the east and Rome in the west. The Parthians enjoyed cordial relations with the Chinese Han dynasty, but their expansion westwards brought them into sharp conflict with Rome. Another source of contention was Armenia, as both Rome and Parthia sought to influence the course of events there. The first

Elevation of a Column Base,
found at
SUSA.
March 1852.

67 Achaemenid column base at Susa, with secondary Greek inscription dating from the Hellenistic period. The letters are cut upside down so that they may be easily read from above. The inscription is a memorial to Arreneides, son of Arreneides, governor of Susa, from his friend Pythagoras, son of Aristarchus.

major encounter between the two powers was at Carrhae (modern Harran in Turkey) in 53BC, which resulted in a decisive defeat for Crassus and his Roman legions. On this occasion the Romans found their infantry no match for the mobile Parthian cavalry commanded by Suren, whose prowess in archery (the so-called 'Parthian shot') has become proverbial. Mark Antony's campaign of 36BC was similarly abortive.

For more than a century thereafter no serious challenge was made to the territorial integrity of Parthia, but this period of comparative quiet was rudely shattered by the aggressive ambitions of Trajan. In his campaign of AD116 this emperor succeeded in capturing Ctesiphon and marching to the shores of the Persian Gulf. Although he soon had to withdraw, from this point onwards Parthia was in decline, racked by internal dissension and threatened externally by the Kushans in the east, the nomadic Alani in the north-west and the Romans in the west. Ctesiphon was sacked twice more, and although there were periods of Parthian revival, notably under Vologases IV in the second half of the second century AD, the state was largely a spent force.

For historical information about the Parthians we are largely dependent on the works of Greek and Latin authors, but generally their accounts are far from objective. Unfortunately, practically nothing the Parthians might have written about themselves has been preserved, but there are inscriptions on coins and on potsherds (ostraca) from sites such as Nysa; in the British Museum is a collection of nearly 200 ostraca with inscriptions in Pahlavi, formerly belonging to E. Herzfeld. Parthian coins are helpful for establishing the succession of kings and their dates, and clay tablets written in cuneiform are a useful source of knowledge about local conditions in Babylonia.

68 Silver coins of the Parthian period: (*top*) tetradrachm of Mithradates I (*c.*171–138BC), minted at Seleucia; (*centre*) drachm of Osroes II (*c.*AD190), minted at Ecbatana; (*bottom*) tetradrachm of Vologases VI (*c.*AD208–28), minted at Seleucia. The coin of Osroes II has an Aramaic inscription on the reverse.

68

Before the establishment of Parthian rule, the urban centres of Mesopotamia and Iran had been subjected to a fairly intensive period of Hellenisation, and naturally this influence did not suddenly disappear with the advent of a new ruling dynasty. Thus, in the early part of the Parthian period, Greek was retained as the official language. Greek cities such as Seleucia were allowed to prosper, and Mithradates I and some of his successors used the epithet 'Philhellene' on their coins. The art of this early period also shows marked Hellenistic influence. This can be seen on the ivory rhyta (drinking-horns) from Nysa, which are mainly decorated with Greek mythological scenes.

Towards the end of the first century BC and certainly in the first century AD, however, the situation began to change and oriental features became more prominent in Parthian culture. A large bronze statue from a sanctuary at Shami, which can be dated to this period by comparison with images on coins, represents a man wearing a Parthian outfit of belted jacket and leggings. His hair hangs in bunches beneath a headband in a characteristic Parthian style. From the first century AD onwards some Hellenistic traits can still be identified, but generally the iconography and composition of works of art are characteristically Parthian. This can be clearly seen in some of the rock-reliefs in western Iran such as Bisitun, Sar-i Pul-i Zohab and Hung-i Nauruzi. They show scenes of investiture, combat and worship with figures dressed in the Parthian costume. Parthian elements can also be found on coins: Aramaic lettering appears for the first time in the reign of Vologases I (AD 51–78).

Evidence for art in the late Parthian period comes mainly from semi-autonomous regional centres such as Elymais in Khuzistan and Hatra in northern Mesopotamia. In Elymais we have the religious centres of Masjid-i Sulaiman and Bard-i Nishandeh, dated to the late second and early third centuries AD, with many reliefs and statues showing worshipping figures. All are represented frontally and most wear the Parthian tunic and trousers. Elsewhere in Elymais there are rock-reliefs of this period at Tang-i Sarvak and Shimbar. At the important site of Hatra, situated on the trans-desert route linking northern Mesopotamia with sites such as Palmyra and Dura Europos in the west, many life-size statues of worshippers have been found in the complex of temples. These detailed representations provide us with much information about the elaborate costumes of this period.

In the realm of architecture there were important developments. During the Parthian period the iwan became a widespread architectural form. This was a great hall, open on one side with a high barrel-vaulted roof, which became a distinctive feature of Parthian monumental buildings. Particularly fine examples have been found at Ashur and Hatra. In the construction of these grandiose halls, fast-setting gypsum mortar was used. Perhaps allied to the increasing use of gypsum mortar at this time is the development of gypsum stucco decoration, also attested in the Hellenistic period at Seleucia. There is particularly lavish use of stucco for wall decoration at Qaleh-i Yazdigird near Qasr-i Shirin in a palace dating from the late Parthian period, and there are some fine examples from Warka and Ashur in Mesopotamia.

Burial practices in the Parthian period were diverse, perhaps testifying to the degree of religious toleration at this time. For example, in the south-western part of the Parthian empire, bodies were often interred in so-called slipper-coffins with oval lids, sometimes elaborately decorated in blue-green glaze. Examples from Warka are decorated with figures of warriors in low relief. Associated with such coffins were a variety of grave-goods including terracotta figurines, coins, vessels in pottery and glass, gold and silver jewellery, crude bone

69 Stone slab with representation of Heracles wearing a diadem or headband with flowing ties and a cloak draped over his shoulders. From Masjid-i Soleiman, a religious terrace-site of ancient Elymais in Khuzistan. Parthian period, late 2nd–early 3rd century AD. Presented to the British Museum by Dr M. Y. Young in 1920. Ht 30.4 cm.

70 (*Right*) Necklace consisting of three oval plaques fixed to a chain. The two plaques showing eagles are inset with turquoise and garnets. Eagles holding rings in their beaks as symbols of kingship are shown both on Parthian coins and rock reliefs. Parthian period, *c.*1st century AD. W (of central plaque) 4.6 cm.

71 (*Above*) Stone slab, probably a lintel from the top of a doorway, found by George Smith at Nineveh in 1874. Although this slab was found in a palace of the Assyrian king Sennacherib (704–681BC), it is clearly Parthian in date. Creatures comparable to the two winged dragons shown, with long sinewy bodies, sometimes appear on the belts of stone statues of the early 3rd century AD from Hatra in northern Mesopotamia.

72 (*Right*) Terracotta plaque showing a reclining male figure holding a cup, probably participating in a banquet. He is wearing the typical Parthian costume of tunic and trousers. 1st–2nd century AD. From Loftus' excavations at Warka in Mesopotamia. L 13.1 cm.

figurines and so on – in short, all those objects which might prove useful to the deceased in the afterlife. Quite different forms of burial, on the other hand, have been attested at Nineveh. Here, bodies were placed in stone coffins, and the faces of the corpses covered with gold masks. A rich selection of jewellery was found with the burials, including a fine pair of earrings set with garnets and turquoise and a large number of small gold plaques that were sewn on to clothing. The wealth of jewellery that must have been in circulation in Parthian times is clear from coin portraits, but unfortunately there are very few examples from excavations. We do, however, have a good range of pottery from Parthian sites, and new and distinctive forms appeared at this time. In the Zagros area of western Iran 'clinky' ware, a hard red pottery which makes a clinky noise when tapped, is a hallmark of the Parthians, whereas in Mesopotamia and Syria blue-green glazed pottery was widespread.

The last Parthian king, Artabanus V, was overthrown about AD224 by Ardashir, a local dynast in Fars whose seat was at Istakhr. He is said to have been a descendant of one Sasan, who gave his name to the Sasanian dynasty founded by Ardashir; the Sasanians were to rule Iran for more than 400 years. They saw themselves as successors to the Achaemenids, after the Hellenistic and Parthian interlude, and perceived it as their role to restore the greatness of Iran. Such ambitions inevitably brought the Sasanian monarchs into conflict with Rome and later Byzantium in the west, and war on that front was to become a constant refrain of Sasanian history. Both sides were motivated by a desire to control the lucrative east-west trade route bringing silks, spices and other luxury goods from the Orient.

In order to create a state that could fulful his grandiose schemes, Ardashir introduced strong central government, reformed the coinage and made Zoroastrianism the state religion. Under

70
73

73 Bronze belt buckle in the form of a horse and rider, the latter with his hair arranged in three bunches, typical of the Parthian period. Decorative buckles showing various compositions, such as couples embracing or animals, were popular in the Parthian period, and a wide range of ornate buckles are shown on the statues from Hatra in northern Mesopotamia. 2nd–3rd century AD. W 7.2 cm.

the Hellenistic and Parthian kings Zoroastrianism had been in decline, and even though the religion was widespread in Achaemenid times it is not certain that the kings themselves were orthodox Zoroastrians. The date of the prophet Zarathustra (Greek Zoroaster) is keenly disputed: he is traditionally regarded as having lived from 628 to 551BC, but some modern scholars believe he flourished in a much earlier period, some time in the second millennium BC. According to his doctrine, a dualistic system existed with opposing forces of good, created by the supreme god Ahuramazda, and evil, symbolised by Ahriman. Other deities such as Anahita and Mithra, whose cult spread across the Roman empire, were regarded as emanations of Ahuramazda. Fire played an important part in Zoroastrian religion, as indicated by the many fire temples (*chahar taq*) surviving from Sasanian times and fire altars shown on Sasanian coins.

The reign of Ardashir's successor Shapur I (AD240–72) is marked by some significant successes against the Romans and the defeat of three Roman emperors, Gordian III, Philip the Arab and Valerian. In addition, Armenia was

74

74 Silver coins of the Sasanian period: (*top*) Ardashir I (AD224–40); (*centre*) Bahram V (AD421–39); (*bottom*) Yazdigird III (AD632–51). Fire altars are shown on the reverse of these coins. Sasanian kings can be distinguished by their distinctive personal crowns.

conquered and the Kushan empire in central Asia was largely overrun. At the end of Shapur's reign the Sasanian empire was at its largest long-term extent, and stretched roughly from the river Euphrates to the Indus. In the north it included Armenia and Georgia and lands up to and probably beyond the river Oxus. Thereafter, though, the empire was constantly changing in size as it reacted to threats on different frontiers.

In religious matters Shapur was remarkably tolerant, and although himself a Zoroastrian he allowed religious minorities to practise freely. He may have had a personal interest in the teachings of the prophet Mani, whose religion combined elements of Zoroastrianism, Christianity and Buddhism. This religious toleration did not last, however, and during the reigns of Shapur's three successors, Bahram I, II and III, all religious minorities but particularly the Manichaeans (who were regarded as heretic by orthodox Zoroastrians) were savagely persecuted. This persecution was orchestrated by Kartir, a priest who wielded enormous power. During this time, also, much territory was lost to the Sasanians. After Bahram III (AD293) minorities were again tolerated, and Jews, Christians, Manichaeans, Mandaeans and Buddhists were all able to practise their religions.

Tangible evidence for the existence of the various sects is found in the pottery incantation bowls, usually dated between the fourth and seventh centuries AD, which have been found particularly in southern Mesopotamia and south-west Iran. The texts are written spirally around the inside of the bowls, and sometimes they have in the centre a crudely drawn figure of a demon. Because when the bowls were found they were often upside down, it seems they were intended to catch – or at least deter – evil spirits. The texts are written in Judaeo-Aramaic, Syriac, Pahlavi or Mandaic.

There are also lead rolls, thin strips of lead inscribed with magical texts and then tightly rolled up. An important group of Mandaic lead rolls, as yet unpublished, is now in the British Museum; they were found in a lead jar in a mound near Qurna in southern Mesopotamia, perhaps Tell Abu Shudhr. The Mandaeans, who wrote a dialect of Aramaic, are sometimes erroneously called 'St John's Christians' because they claim descent from St John the Baptist, but their religion contains elements from various sources including gnosticism.

During the long reign of Shapur II (AD309–79), Sasanian fortunes were to a large extent restored. His campaigns against the Romans were graphically described by Ammianus Marcellinus, a Greek from Antioch in the Roman army; on the whole these were successful, although in AD359 Julian the Apostate managed to reach Ctesiphon. To pay for his military activities Shapur had to levy heavy taxes, and the Christians, who had been persecuted since Constantine converted to Christianity and made it the official religion of the Roman empire, bore the brunt of these. During Shapur's reign the Zoroastrian holy book, the Avesta, was written down in Middle Persian, the language of the Sasanian period, using the Aramaic script.

After the reign of Shapur II, the Sasanians were increasingly beset with problems on their northern and eastern frontiers. These were caused by various nomadic groups, particularly the Hephthalite Huns in central Asia, to whom the Sasanians were forced to pay an annual tribute. These problems were compounded by drought and famine and by the disruptive message of a new prophet, Mazdak, who advocated a form of communism. This was incompatible with the rigid hierarchical system of Sasanian society, which was divided into four classes – priests, warriors, scribes and common people – between which it was practically impossible to move.

There was a Sasanian renaissance under Chosroes I Anushirvan (AD531–79). This energetic monarch, whose name means 'of the immortal soul', completed a detailed survey of resources within the empire, a sort of Domesday Book, and used it to reform the taxation system. With the increased revenue he was able to maintain a paid army – previously the feudal barons had provided soldiers out of their own resources – and undertake major irrigation works that resulted in a great increase in agricultural productivity. During his long reign he defeated the Hephthalites and was successful in the long-standing struggle with Byzantium. After a period of internal unrest and dynastic squabbling in Iran, Chosroes II (AD591–628) renewed the conflict and overran much of the Near East. He even captured Jerusalem, carrying off what was said to be the 'true cross'.

The splendour in which the Sasanian monarchs lived is well illustrated by their surviving palaces, such as those at Firuzabad and Bishapur in Fars, and the capital city of Ctesiphon in Mesopotamia. All are characterised by the barrel-vaulted iwans introduced in the Parthian period, but now they reached massive proportions, particularly at Ctesiphon. An innovation of the Sasanian period was the construction of domes built up from squinches in the corners of square rooms. Such domes could be built where barrel vaults enclosed a square space. At Bishapur some of the floors were decorated with mosaics showing scenes of merrymaking as at a banquet; the Roman influence here is clear, and the mosaics may have been laid by Roman prisoners. Stucco wall decoration also appears at Bishapur, but better examples are preserved from Chal Tarkhan near Rayy (late Sasanian or early Islamic in date), and from Ctesiphon and Kish in Mesopotamia. The panels variously show animal figures set in roundels, human busts, and geometric and floral motifs. Buildings

75

75 (*Right*) Moulded stucco plaque, showing a *senmurw*, a mythical creature with the foreparts of a dog or lion, and the wings and tail of a bird. From Chal Tarkhan near Rayy. Late Sasanian or early Islamic, 7th–8th century AD. Ht 16.9 cm.

76 (*Below*) Rock relief at Taq-i Bustan showing the investiture of the Sasanian king Ardashir II (AD 379–83). The king (centre) is given a royal diadem by Ahuramazda, while Mithra stands behind the king in a supporting role.

were also decorated with wall-paintings; particularly fine examples have been found at Kuh-i Khwaja in Sistan. Other notable Sasanian sites include Takht-i Suleiman in Azerbaijan, where an important fire temple and palace were built around a supposedly bottomless lake; the tower at Paikuli in Iraqi Kurdistan, with long inscriptions of King Narseh (AD293–302); and the temple at Kangavar, dedicated to Anahita.

But the best-known monuments of the Sasanian period are the rock-reliefs carved by nearly all Sasanian kings from Ardashir to Shapur III (AD383–8) and then again by Chosroes II (AD591–628). There are fine examples at Bishapur, Firuzabad, Naqsh-i Rustam, Naqsh-i Rajab (a small grotto near Istakhr), and Taq-i Bustan near Kermanshah. Most common are investiture scenes, showing the king being given the right to rule by a deity, normally Ahuramazda. In these the deity hands over a diadem or headband with flowing ribbons, clearly a type of head-dress symbolic of kingship. Another frequent theme in the reliefs is victory over the Romans, with Shapur I recording his successes no less than four times. In two reliefs at Bishapur the central panel probably shows the victorious Sasanian king on horseback, trampling the body of Gordian. Before him kneels Philip the Arab, while Valerian is standing submissively behind the king. On either side of these central panels are additional registers showing Sasanian troops and tribute-bearers.

But the most remarkable Sasanian reliefs are at Taq-i Bustan. Here a king, probably Chosroes II, carved an iwan out of the rock. On the back wall is an investiture scene with the king on horseback below; the side walls show the king hunting wild boar and deer.

Amongst the small antiquities of Sasanian date, the silver vessels, particularly bowls, are well known. There are fine collections in a number of museums, especially the State

77 Iwan carved out of a cliff at Taq-i Bustan, probably by Chosroes II (AD591–628). The relief decoration on the back wall shows at the top an investiture scene, with the king standing between Ahuramazda and Anahita, while at the bottom the king appears on horseback, dressed in full armour and a helmet through which only his eyes are visible. Here is an obvious forerunner of the knights of medieval Europe. Drawing by Sir Robert Ker Porter. British Library Add. MS 14758(ii) 113/128.

78 The relief on one of the side walls of the iwan at Taq-i Bustan, showing a royal boar hunt in a swamp. The king, probably Chosroes II (AD591–628), armed with a bow, stands in a boat in the centre. The dead boars are loaded on to elephants. On the opposite wall of the iwan a deer hunt is shown. Drawing by Sir Robert Ker Porter. British Library Add. MS 14758(ii) 114/129.

Hermitage in Leningrad. Many of these bowls come from those parts of central Asia that are now in the Soviet Union. Just as the silver was distributed over a wide geographical area, so it has a wide chronological range; some of the vessels, though they are in Sasanian style, seem to date from the early Islamic period. Hunting scenes are particularly popular on these bowls, showing that this was a popular pastime of the Sasanian kings, but also common is a central design of a bird set in a roundel. Vessels showing banqueting scenes are less typically Sasanian and owe more to western influence.

Another characteristic product of the Sasanian period are the stamp seals, of which great numbers are known. The designs are engraved on a variety of attractive coloured stones and range from busts of the king, often accompanied by an inscription in Middle Persian, to animal portraits, fire altars and floral motifs. Luxury goods of all kinds abounded in the Sasanian empire, and there is increasing evidence for the extensive use of elaborately decorated textiles, particularly silk. Sasanian silks were treasured far beyond Iran – they have been identified in Europe, Egypt, central Asia and Chinese Turkestan. There was also a tradition of fine glassware. The pottery is not as well known as it should be, but it is clear there were a number of regional variations. In northern Mesopotamia, for example, pottery stamped with various kinds of animal and geometric designs has been found at a number of sites.

In AD637 disaster overtook the Sasanians. They were defeated at Qadisiya near Ctesiphon by an Arab army filled with the crusading zeal

79 (Right) Silver gilt vase pierced like a colander at the base, with scenes showing a grape harvest. Two naked cherub-like boys gather grapes, while between the vines birds and foxes are trying to steal the fruit. The inspiration for this sort of decoration is classical, based on the cult of Dionysos. There is a partly legible Pahlevi inscription on the rim. Sasanian, 6th–7th century AD. Ht 18.5 cm.

of Islam. A further reverse followed at Nahavand in AD642, and the last Sasanian king
74 Yazdigird III (AD632–51) was forced to flee the
battle; he was eventually murdered at Merv.
So ended Sasanian rule in Iran, and the
82 Islamic era began. The reasons for the sudden
collapse of the Sasanian empire are not clear.
However, one important factor must be that
the Arabs had previously made inroads into
Mesopotamia, but their potential threat was
largely ignored. Also, by the mid-seventh
century the Sasanian state must have been
exhausted by its long years of struggle with
Rome and Byzantium, and oppressive taxation
coupled with a rigid class system would have
made Islam seem an attractive alternative to
many disaffected subjects of the great king.

80 (*Below*) Silver gilt dish showing a *senmerw*, the creature that appears on a stucco plaque
75. Sasanian, 7th century AD. Presented to the British Museum by the National Art
Collections Fund in 1922. D 19.3 cm.

82 (*Right*) Monstrous bronze figure, allegedly found near the Helmand River in Afghanistan. Fantastic creatures such as these dragons are often depicted in Sasanian art, and are also found on the stone façade of the Islamic palace at Mshaṭṭā in Jordan, dating from *c.*740AD. 7th–8th century AD. Ht 24.9 cm.

81 (*Below*) Pottery jar with stamped designs from Borsippa in Mesopotamia. Pottery with stamped designs showing animals, crosses and geometric shapes has been found at a number of sites in northern Mesopotamia and is characteristic of the late Sasanian period, *c.*6th century AD. Ht 33.5 cm.

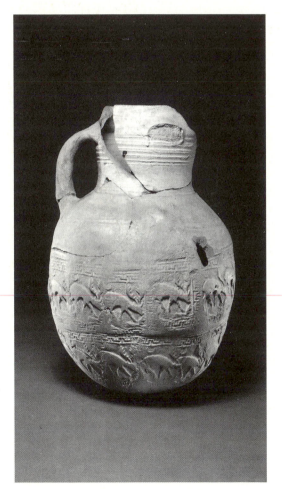

83 (*Right*) Impression from a large carnelian seal showing, according to the Pahlevi inscription, Vehdin-Shapur, the chief storekeeper of Iran. He is thought to have been an official under Yazdigird II (AD439–57), and his rank is shown by the elaborate head-dress. 4.6 × 3.8 cm.

9 The discovery of ancient Persia

Although the Sasanians were overthrown in the seventh century AD, their art and institutions were to survive for a longer period. Sasanian influence is everywhere to be seen in Islamic art, ranging from the standard mosque plan derived from the Sasanian iwan and dome to Sasanian motifs on pottery of the tenth and eleventh centuries at Nishapur. This influence was not confined to the east but extended into Byzantium. Many of the institutions of the Sasanians, such as their administrative and legal systems, were taken over in part by the Arab conquerors and, as we have seen, a number of distinctively Sasanian works of art – for example, some of the silver bowls – should be dated to the early Islamic period.

Nor were the achievements of the Sasanians forgotten in Iran, where legends about them abounded. Their exploits are recorded – usually fancifully, with little regard to historical fact – in a number of literary works and in Persian miniatures, most notably in the Persian national epic the *Shahnameh* written by Ferdowsi in the eleventh century AD.

But for all their interest in the Sasanians, later writers knew practically nothing of the glories of the Achaemenid period, and although Alexander the Great was remembered, he was turned into the half-brother of Darius III. This almost complete ignorance of the Achaemenid period in Iran was in sharp contrast to Europe, where tradition was preserved not only through classical authors but also in the Bible. In Iran, interest in the Achaemenid kings and their Parthian and Sasanian successors revived in the nineteenth century under the Qajar kings, when it became fashionable to make copies of Achae-

84 Persian miniature from a *Khamsa* of Nizami, illuminated between 1539 and 1543 for Shah Tahmasp. In this scene the folk hero Bahram Gur, who can be identified with the Sasanian king Bahram V (AD421–39) in 74 (*centre*), is shown hunting lions. The composition is similar to that found on a number of silver bowls of the Sasanian period. British Library Or. MS 2265, f.202b.

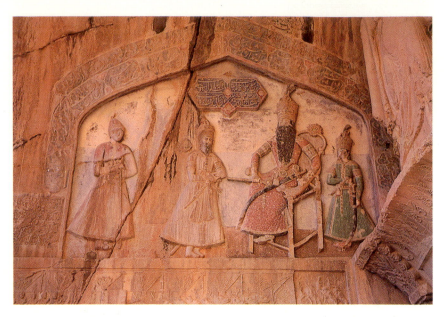

85 Relief at Taq-i Bustan, carved in Qajar times in imitation of ancient rock reliefs and showing the Persian king Fath 'Ali Shah (1797–1835).

monuments. Nor should we forget A. H. Layard, the excavator of Nimrud and Nineveh, who journeyed through parts of Persia in the early 1840s, or H. C. Rawlinson, whose work on the Bisitun inscriptions has been described earlier (p.39). Another influential figure was the Hon. George Curzon, later viceroy of India, whose *Persia and the Persian Question* (1892), written as a political analysis of what was considered to be an area crucial to British interests, remains a mine of information of every sort about Iran.

In spite of the keen interest of these Victorian and earlier travellers, there was relatively little archaeological activity in Iran. The excavations of W. K. Loftus at Susa have been described (p.13), but such enterprises were few and far between. Then, following a visit to Iran in 1889, Jacques de Morgan extracted from Nasr-ed Din Shah a concession for the French to do archaeological excavations not only at Susa but throughout Persia. Thus most of the archaeological work before the Second World War was done by French teams.

In the 1960s and 1970s, however, there was a tremendous increase in archaeological activity, with expeditions from many countries including Britain, the United States, France, Germany, Canada, Italy, Belgium and Denmark, as well as a considerable input from the Iranians themselves. During this period many important sites were excavated, such as Hasanlu, Marlik, Susa, Pasargadae, Shahdad, Tepe Yahya and Shahr-i Sokhteh, and great strides forward were made in our knowledge about ancient Iran. Since the Islamic revolution in 1979 this work has practically come to a stop, but it is to be hoped that it will be resumed in the not-too-distant future. There are undoubtedly exciting discoveries yet to be made, and there is still much to be learnt about ancient Persia, one of the most fascinating and splendid civilisations of the ancient world.

menid reliefs for country-house ornaments, and rock reliefs were carved in ancient style.

The existence of the magnificent ruins at Persepolis was known to European travellers as early as the fourteenth century, and the Elizabethan playwright Christopher Marlowe refers to Persepolis in his famous play *Tamburlaine*. In the following centuries various intrepid Europeans – first a trickle and then in greater numbers during the eighteenth and nineteenth centuries – visited these and other ruins and recorded their impressions for posterity. Amongst the British travellers whose records have proved to be of lasting value may be counted James Morier (1780–1849), who is chiefly remembered not for his valuable travelogues but for his brilliantly witty and amusing classic, *The Adventures of Hajji Baba of Ispahan* (1824). Then there was Sir Robert Ker Porter, a professional artist, who was commissioned by an influential patron in St Petersburg (Leningrad) to visit Iran in 1817–19 to make studies and drawings of sculptures and

85

contents page

42, 43, 77, 78

Further reading

Pierre Amiet, *L'âge des échanges inter-iraniens 3500–1700 avant J.-C.* (Paris 1986).

Elizabeth Carter and Matthew W. Stolper, *Elam: Surveys of Political History and Archaeology* (Berkeley, California 1984).

M. A. R. Colledge, *Parthian Art* (London 1977).

O. M. Dalton, *The Treasure of the Oxus* (3rd edn, London 1964).

Richard N. Frye, *History of Ancient Iran* (Munich 1984).

Roman Ghirshman, *Iran: Parthians and Sasanians* (London 1962).

Roman Ghirshman, *Persia from the Origins to Alexander the Great* (London 1964).

Prudence Oliver Harper, *The Royal Hunter: Art of the Sasanian Empire* (New York 1978).

Georgina Herrmann, *The Iranian Revival* (Oxford 1977).

Sylvia A. Matheson, *Persia: An Archaeological Guide* (London 1976).

P. R. S. Moorey, *Catalogue of the Ancient Persian Bronzes in the Ashmolean Museum* (Oxford 1971).

E. Porada, *Ancient Iran* (London 1965).

Michael Roaf, *Sculptures and Sculptors at Persepolis* (Iran XXI, London 1983).

Margaret Cool Root, *The King and Kingship in Achaemenid Art* (Acta Iranica 19, Leiden 1979).

David Stronach, *Pasargadae* (Oxford 1978).

L. Vanden Berghe, *Archéologie de l'Iran Ancien* (Leiden 1959).

Much of the literature about ancient Iran, particularly concerning modern excavations, is in the form of articles in periodicals such as *Iran*, the journal of the British Institute of Persian Studies. The relevant chapters in *The Cambridge History of Iran* and *The Cambridge Ancient History* are also useful.

Rulers of Iran 550BC–AD651

Achaemenids

Cyrus	550–530BC
Cambyses	530–522
Bardiya	522
Darius I	522–486
Xerxes	486–465
Artaxerxes I	465–424
Xerxes II	424–423
Darius II	423–404
Artaxerxes II	404–359
Artaxerxes III	359–338
Arses	338–336
Darius III	336–331

Macedonian/Seleucids

Alexander the Great	331–323
Seleucus I	312–281
Antiochus I	281–261
Antiochus II	261–246
Seleucus II	246–226
Seleucus III	226–223
Antiochus III	223–187
Seleucus IV	187–175

Parthians

Arsaces	c.238–211
Artabanus I	c.211–191
Priapatius	c.191–176
Phraates I	c.176–171
Mithradates I	c.171–138
Phraates II	c.138–127
Artabanus II	c.127–124
Mithradates II	c.123–88
Gotarzes I	c.95–90
Orodes I	c.90–80
Sinatruces	c.75
Phraates III	c.70–57
Mithradates III	c.57–54
Orodes II	c.57–38
Pacorus I	c.39
Phraates IV	c.38–2
Tiridates	c.29–27
Phraataces	c.2BC–AD4
Orodes III	c.AD6
Vonones I	c.8–12
Artabanus III	c.10–38
Vardanes I	c.40–45
Gotarzes II	c.40–51
Vonones II	c.51
Vologases I	c.51–78
Vardanes II	c.55–58
Vologases II	c.77–80
Pacorus II	c.78–105
Artabanus IV	c.80–90
Vologases III	c.105–147
Osroes I	c.109–129
Parthamaspates	c.116
Mithradates IV	c.140
Vologases IV	c.147–191
Osroes II	c.190
Vologases V	c.191–208
Vologases VI	c.208–228
Artabanus V	c.216–224

Sasanians

Ardashir I	224–240
Shapur I	240–272
Hormuzd I	272–273
Bahram I	273–276
Bahram II	276–293
Bahram III	293
Narseh	293–302
Hormuzd II	302–309
Shapur II	309–379
Ardashir II	379–383
Shapur III	383–388
Bahram IV	388–399
Yazdigird I	399–421
Bahram V	421–439
Yazdigird II	439–457
Hormuzd III	457–459
Peroz	459–484
Valash	484–488
Kavad I	488–531
Chosroes I	531–579
Hormuzd IV	579–590
Bahram VI	590–591
Chosroes II	591–628
Kavad II	628
Ardashir III	628–629
Purandokht	629–630
Hormuzd V	c.630–631
Chosroes III	c.631–632
Yazdigird III	632–651

British Museum registration numbers

Front cover	WA 123908
Inside front cover	129381
Title page	124091
3	1924-9-2,2
4	128622
6	116455
7	123277-8
8	123268
10	120929
13	113886
14	91823, 91833, 53-12-19,24
15	53-12-19,42
16	132960
17	132225
18	134906-7
19	134387
20	136794
21	132819-20
22	129072
24	129984, 136110-3, 136120-1
26	132825
27	134383-4
29	123276
30	130677
31	123542
32	108816
33	132900, 132927
34	122190
35	130676
36	131072
37	135755
40	135072-85
47	118845
48	118838
52	118868
53	118839
55	140671
56	89132
57	134740
58	135571
59	124081
60	123923
61	123949
62	124017
63	123905
64	123901
65	123918
66	123906
69	127335
70	134628
71	118896
72	91786
73	139205
75	135913
79	124094
80	124095
81	92394
82	123267
83	119994
Inside back cover	123924
Back cover	132525

Index

Figures in italic refer to illustration numbers